I LUV MY FERRARI

SANTANU SAXENAA

INDIA • SINGAPORE • MALAYSIA

ISBN
Paperback 979-8-89588-610-6
Hardcase 979-8-89724-266-5

जय श्री गणेश!

वक्रतुण्ड महाकाय सूर्यकोटि समप्रभ।

निर्विघ्नं कुरु मे देव सर्वकार्येषु सर्वदा॥

Vakra-Tunndda Maha-Kaaya Suurya-Kotti Samaprabha|

Nirvighnam Kuru Me Deva Sarva-Kaaryessu Sarvadaa||

(Salutations to Sri Ganesha)

Who has a Curved Trunk, Who has a Large Body and
whose Splendor is similar to Million Suns;

O Deva, Please Make My Undertakings Free of
Obstacles, By Extending Your Blessings in All My
Works, Always.

Contents

Epilogue

Foreword

In the bustling symphony of modern life, where the rhythm of ambition often drowns out the whispers of inner peace, finding a harmonious balance can seem like an elusive quest. Many of us are familiar with the dichotomy presented by spiritual teachings: the notion that true peace is only attainable through renunciation and detachment. Yet, **what if I told you that you could achieve profound inner tranquility without abandoning your passions, possessions, or the very life you cherish?**

This is precisely the transformative journey explored in **'I Luv My Ferrari'**. In this compelling narrative, we follow Aryan Kapoor, a man whose life epitomizes success and luxury. Aryan is not just a wealthy individual; he is a living embodiment of ambition, achievement, and material prosperity. However, his journey is not merely about accumulating wealth or flaunting success—it is about reconciling these external markers with a deep, abiding inner peace.

The beauty of Aryan's story lies in its departure from the conventional paths of spiritual exploration. While traditional wisdom often suggests that true enlightenment requires a retreat from the world, Aryan's journey demonstrates a different approach. He shows us that one need not forsake their material success to attain spiritual fulfillment. Instead, peace and mindfulness can be cultivated within the very context of a high-paced, ambitious lifestyle.

As you delve into the chapters of this book, you will witness Aryan's evolution from a driven achiever to a balanced individual who integrates his worldly desires with spiritual growth. Each chapter offers valuable insights and practical wisdom, drawing from both ancient teachings and modern perspectives. From embracing material wealth without attachment to practicing mindfulness amidst the chaos of everyday life, Aryan's experiences offer a fresh perspective on achieving inner peace.

In this narrative, the teachings from The Monk Who Sold His Ferrari and the timeless wisdom of the Bhagavad Gita serve as guiding lights, illuminating Aryan's path. The book is a rich tapestry of personal anecdotes, philosophical reflections, and transformative lessons, all woven together to reveal a profound truth: that peace is not a distant goal but a present reality accessible in every moment, regardless of external circumstances.

'I Luv My Ferrari' invites readers to embark on a journey of their own. It challenges the conventional wisdom that spiritual fulfillment requires sacrifice and separation from the material world. Instead, it offers a compelling argument that balance, mindfulness, and perspective can lead to the same profound inner peace that others find through renunciation.

As you turn these pages, may you find inspiration in Aryan's journey and discover that the path to peace can indeed be woven into the fabric of your daily life.

Whether you are a seeker of wisdom, a lover of luxury, or someone striving for balance in a fast-paced world, this book holds valuable lessons for everyone.

The destination of inner peace is not reserved for the few who renounce everything but is accessible to all who seek it with an open heart and a balanced mind.

– Santanu Saxenaa

Introduction: The Unlikely Seeker

"Why would anyone give up the world when they could conquer it?"

This question wasn't just a passing thought for Aryan; it was a mantra that had helped drive every decision that he made. Being a man of ambition, Aryan wasn't just another success story—he was the definition of success itself. His life was a blueprint for everything society revered: wealth, power, status, and a relentless pursuit of more. And Aryan loved every second of it.

On any given day, you could hear the purr of his red Ferrari cutting through the city streets, a beast of a machine that reflected his life in the fast lane. The car wasn't just transportation—it was a statement, a roar to the world that Aryan had made it. His sleek suits, designer watches, and penthouse overlooking the shimmering skyline were symbols of a man who had climbed the mountain of success and planted his flag at the summit. To everyone around him, Aryan was the epitome of modern ambition.

But in the quiet moments, away from the noise, there was a different story playing out inside Aryan's mind—a story he never dared to speak aloud.

Why, with everything I've achieved, does something still feel incomplete?

From the outside, Aryan's life looked perfect. He had built an empire, one deal at a time, watching his wealth multiply while his competitors crumbled. He wasn't just living the dream; he was the dream—a man whose very presence radiated confidence, control, and charm. His calendar was packed with high-profile meetings, exclusive events, and spontaneous getaways to the most luxurious destinations in the world.

In a world where success was the ultimate currency, Aryan was as rich as they came.

But lately, there was a whisper inside him, a subtle but persistent voice that he couldn't quite shake. It wasn't loud, but it was there—growing louder with each passing day. It came at night, when the city lights twinkled below his penthouse, and he stood alone on his balcony with a glass of whiskey in hand.

The view was breathtaking, but the satisfaction was fleeting.

Watching Others Walk Away

Aryan wasn't the kind of man who doubted himself—at least, that's what he liked to believe. But recently, something had started to stir inside him. He began noticing a curious trend among his peers—successful men and women, just like him, who had reached the pinnacle of success and then… walked away. They weren't just taking sabbaticals or vacations; they were **renouncing it all**. Selling their homes, abandoning their Ferraris, and retreating to faraway places to meditate and 'find themselves'.

Take Raj, for example. Raj had been one of the most driven, ambitious people Aryan knew. They'd built their careers alongside one another, competing, collaborating, and thriving in the business world. But Raj had shocked everyone when he suddenly sold his company, packed his bags, and moved to a remote village to live a simple life. When they met for coffee before Raj left, Aryan couldn't believe what he was hearing.

"Inner peace?" Aryan had laughed, shaking his head. **"You've got everything a man could want, and you're giving it all up? Why would you do that to yourself?"**

Raj had smiled—a calm, knowing smile that bothered Aryan more than he cared to admit. **"You 'll understand one day,"** Raj had said. **"It's not about what you have. It's about what you're missing."**

At the time, Aryan had dismissed it as nonsense. Raj was just going through a phase, a mid-life crisis disguised as spiritual awakening. But then, Raj wasn't the only one. More and more people in Aryan's circle were taking this path—selling their luxury items, scaling back their careers, and embracing simplicity in search of something Aryan couldn't quite put his finger on.

What were they searching for that Aryan hadn't found?

Aryan scoffed at the very idea of renouncing luxury. **Why should anyone have to give up the world to find**

happiness? He couldn't understand it. His Ferrari was more than just a car—it was the reward for years of hard work, the symbol of every victory he had fought for. His penthouse wasn't just a home—it was his sanctuary, a fortress built with ambition and sweat. Why would he give that up for something as intangible as 'inner peace'?

The idea was laughable to Aryan. He had always believed that **success and happiness were intertwined**— that the more he achieved, the happier he would be. And for the most part, he was right. There was an undeniable rush that came with closing a major deal, the satisfaction of seeing his company's profits soar, the thrill of living a life that most people could only dream of.

But there were cracks in the foundation – cracks that were becoming harder to ignore.

The Whisper of Doubt

Late at night, Aryan would find himself staring out at the city from his penthouse balcony, the lights stretching as far as the eye could see. It was in these moments—when the world was quiet, and the only sound was the distant hum of traffic—that the whispers began.

"What If Raj Was Right?"

It was a question that gnawed at Aryan, despite his best efforts to ignore it. What if there was something more? What if all the success, the wealth, the accolades—what if none of it mattered if he couldn't find peace within himself?

He didn't want to believe it. He wasn't ready to give up everything he had worked for. But the more he thought about it, the more he realized that **inner peace didn't have to come from renunciation.**

Wasn't It Possible to Have Both?

The Unlikely Seeker

For Aryan, the idea of selling everything and retreating to a quiet life was out of the question. He couldn't imagine living without the luxuries he had come to enjoy. His Ferrari wasn't just a car; it was a part of him. His penthouse wasn't just a place to sleep; it was a symbol of his success. And yet, he couldn't deny that the idea of **inner peace** intrigued him.

The more he thought about it, the more he began to wonder:

Could it be possible to achieve spiritual fulfillment without giving up worldly success?

Was there a way to master the material world without being enslaved by it?

What if the key to happiness wasn't in renunciation, but in mastery?

Ø What if one didn't have to choose between the material and the spiritual, but could instead learn to thrive in both?

Aryan didn't have the answers, but he knew one thing for certain—he wasn't about to follow in Raj's footsteps. He wasn't going to sell his possessions or walk away from his empire. But maybe, just maybe, he could find a way to balance it all.

Aryan wasn't ready to give up his life of luxury. But he was ready to start asking the hard questions. And in that moment, as he stood on his balcony overlooking the world he had conquered, Aryan took the first step on a journey he never thought he would take—the journey of an unlikely seeker, one who would attempt to find peace not by abandoning the world, but by embracing it fully.

Chapter 1

Life of Unapologetic Success

Aryan Kapoor was not just a man of success—he was the very embodiment of ambition. His rise to the top was the stuff of legends, a tale woven with sheer determination, focus, and an unshakable belief in his own potential. The world watched in awe as he scaled the corporate heights, amassing wealth that spoke volumes about his relentless pursuit of greatness. But Aryan didn't just chase success— he reveled in it.

For him, materialism wasn't a distraction; it was a celebration of his triumphs. His lavish penthouse, perched above the glittering city, wasn't just a home—it was a monument to his achievements, a testament to the long nights and sacrifices that had fueled his meteoric rise. Every object in his life—his Ferrari, his designer suits, the exotic vacations—wasn't just a possession. Each was a reward, a milestone in his journey. And why should he feel guilty? "Success is not to be measured by what you accomplish, but by the opposition you have encountered, and the courage with which you have maintained the struggle against overwhelming odds," as Orison Swett Marden once said. Aryan embodied this belief, unapologetic in his pursuit of his ambition.

"Why give up the world when you can master it?"

The very idea that one should relinquish their hard-earned luxuries for some higher purpose seemed absurd to Aryan. He had built his empire brick by brick, with blood, sweat, and resolve. Why should he renounce it now? The Ferrari in his garage, the penthouse filled with fine art, the private jet at his disposal—these weren't distractions. They were a reflection of his journey, his relentless commitment to excellence. In Aryan's mind, success didn't need to come at the cost of enlightenment. He could have both.

As Ayn Rand once said, "The question isn't who is going to let me; it's who is going to stop me." And Aryan had lived his life by that mantra. No force could convince him to walk away from the life he had built. Yet, there was a growing whisper in the back of his mind—a whisper that questioned whether this success, however grand, was enough.

The Dilemma of the Material World

As Aryan navigated through the city's twinkling lights, he found himself grappling with a new dilemma. The glitz and glamour that had once been the pinnacle of his existence now seemed to clash with the notion of inner peace. Could he truly have it all—living in luxury while also finding spiritual fulfillment?

The idea of letting go of everything he had worked for seemed inconceivable. The Ferrari, the penthouse, the designer suits—these were not just symbols of his success; they were his identity. The thought of abandoning them for a quest for inner peace felt like betraying himself. Yet, the prospect of discovering a deeper sense of fulfillment was undeniably appealing.

Aryan began to ponder the possibility of balancing his materialistic desires with a search for spiritual enlightenment. Could he enjoy the fruits of his labor while also nurturing his soul? The challenge was not to escape from his world but to find a way to integrate it with a deeper sense of purpose.

The thought of inner tranquility, of a deeper sense of fulfillment that went beyond material success, tugged at him like a distant memory. It wasn't that Aryan wanted to give up his wealth; it was the gnawing realization that perhaps there was something more—something deeper he had yet to uncover. Could he really strike a balance? As Oscar Wilde once said, "Everything in moderation, including moderation."

The Search for Balance

Aryan's inner conflict grew more intense. Was it really necessary to choose between luxury and enlightenment, or was there a way to blend the two? His mind was caught between two worlds—the shimmering allure of materialism and the quieter, more profound pull of spiritual fulfillment. The more he pondered, the more he realized the answer wasn't in renouncing his success but in learning to live within it while nurturing his soul.

He began to see his life as an experiment—could he enjoy the fruits of his labor while also cultivating inner peace? Aryan realized that his journey didn't have to be about leaving behind the material world but learning to transcend it. The challenge was no longer about giving up what he had, but finding a way to integrate his achievements with a deeper sense of purpose.

"The only thing worse than being blind is having sight but no vision," said Helen Keller, and Aryan had a vision. He didn't want to live as a monk, disconnected from the world. He wanted to thrive in it, to live in harmony with both his outer and inner worlds. The Ferrari he now had wasn't just another trophy—it was a symbol of how far he had come and how far he could still go. Aryan's quest wasn't to renounce wealth, but to master it, to drive toward a life where success and spirituality coexisted.

The thrill wasn't in giving up; it was in finding balance, in living life fully and unapologetically. As he stood at the crossroads of his journey, Aryan understood that true mastery lay not in abandoning the material, but in transcending its limitations. This was the next phase of his evolution—the art of being both a monk and a millionaire, unapologetic in his pursuit of both wealth and wisdom. *The question wasn't whether he could have it all; the question was how. And Aryan was ready to find the answer.*

A New Path

As he steered his Ferrari onto the winding deserted road, Aryan felt an electrifying surge of excitement. He was about to embark on a journey that promised to be as thrilling and unpredictable as his rise to success. The hum of the engine beneath him echoed the beating of his heart—steady, but filled with the promise of something more. The open road stretched out before him like an invitation, the horizon bathed in the golden glow of a fading sunset, as if the universe itself was signaling a new beginning. His grip on the wheel tightened, not out of fear, but in readiness for the unknown. This journey, unlike the countless others he had taken, wasn't about speed or arriving at a particular destination—it was about the road itself.

The road ahead was uncertain and the landscape unpredictable, yet there was a strange comfort in the uncertainty.

As the Ferrari purred through the empty streets, Aryan realized that his excitement wasn't rooted in the thrill of speed, but in the possibilities that lay beyond each curve. There was a quiet whisper in his mind, a question that had begun to take shape during his moments of reflection: Could life's greatest meaning be found not in what he had achieved, but in what he had yet to discover?

A quote from Steve Jobs echoed in his mind, one he had often dismissed as idealistic: *"Your work is going to fill a large part of your life, and the only way to be truly satisfied is to do what you believe is great work. And the only way to do great work is to love what you do."* Aryan had always loved the grind, the thrill of building empires. But for the first time, he questioned whether the work he had poured his life into could evolve into something greater—something that aligned with the deeper meaning he was now seeking.

The Journey Continues

The city lights blurred past as Aryan drove, his thoughts racing with anticipation. What would this new path reveal? Could he find a way to live fully in both realms—luxury and spirituality? The journey ahead was a canvas of endless possibilities, and Aryan was ready to paint it with the colors of both his material and spiritual aspirations.

As the Ferrari roared through the night, Aryan's resolve hardened. He was ready to explore this new path with the same fervor that had driven his success. This was not just a quest for inner peace but an adventure to redefine what it meant to live a truly successful life. As the headlights illuminated the next bend, Aryan knew that this journey had just begun, and he was eager to see where it would lead.

Chapter 2

The First Doubts

The sky was painted in hues of orange and pink as Aryan Kapoor sat on the terrace of his lavish penthouse. The soft hum of the city below was a familiar soundtrack, blending with the gentle clink of ice in his crystal glass. It had been another victorious day—a multi-million-dollar deal secured, the latest luxury watch added to his collection, and, as always, his prized Ferrari gleaming in the garage. Life was perfect, a mirror of everything Aryan had dreamed of since he was young. Success, fame, luxury—he had it all. Or so he thought.

But tonight, something felt different. The satisfaction that typically accompanied his achievements seemed fleeting. There was a quiet unease creeping in—a whisper of doubt that had been growing louder, lingering just beneath the surface of his thoughts. It was an unsettling feeling, one he hadn't experienced before. Aryan, the man who always knew what he wanted, found himself questioning it all.

As he swirled the amber liquid in his glass, he gazed out at the sprawling cityscape, where skyscrapers rose like symbols of ambition, the very essence of his life. Yet now, amidst the beauty of the setting sun and the view of his empire, the satisfaction felt hollow.

Why? he wondered, unsettled by the thought. He had everything—so why did it suddenly feel like something was missing?

Before he could sink further into his thoughts, his phone buzzed. A message popped up on the screen. It was from Raj, an old college friend he hadn't spoken to in months.

"In town for a few days. Let's catch up?"

Aryan stared at the message for a moment, feeling a pang of nostalgia. Raj had once walked a similar path—just as ambitious, just as determined to conquer the world. But a few years ago, Raj had done something Aryan still couldn't fully understand—he had walked away from it all. The corporate job, the luxury apartment, the desire for more. Raj had traded it for a minimalist life, focused on simplicity and inner peace.

It had baffled Aryan at the time. Why would anyone, after reaching the pinnacle of success, willingly step away from it? Why would someone abandon a life of luxury for… nothing? Aryan had brushed it off then, thinking Raj had taken the easy way out, running from the pressures of the real world. But tonight, as the lingering unease swirled inside him, Aryan felt a strange pull to see his old friend.

"Sure," Aryan typed back. "Let's meet tomorrow."

The next morning, Aryan found himself in a quaint little café, far removed from the places he usually frequented. No gleaming glass windows, no valet service, just the simple charm of a neighborhood joint. The kind of place Raj would choose. As Aryan waited, sipping a latte, he caught himself looking at his surroundings—a world so different from his own, yet peaceful in its simplicity.

Raj arrived shortly after, looking relaxed in simple, comfortable clothes, a stark contrast to Aryan's crisp designer suit. Raj's face carried a calmness that seemed almost unnatural to Aryan, who was used to the sharp, intense energy of the business world.

"Long time," Raj said with a warm smile as he sat down. His demeanor was easy, content, as if he had found something Aryan hadn't.

"Yeah, it's been a while," Aryan replied, forcing a smile, though part of him couldn't help but feel a little uneasy. There was something different about Raj now, something that unsettled him. He couldn't quite put his finger on it.

They exchanged pleasantries, catching up on the surface-level details of their lives. Raj talked about his quiet, simple life in a small town, his days spent hiking and meditating, and the joy he found in minimalism. Aryan spoke of his thriving business, his latest investments, and his growing collection of luxury cars. But as the conversation wore on, Aryan found himself growing restless.

He leaned forward, unable to hold back his curiosity any longer. "So, Raj," Aryan began, his tone curious but tinged with disbelief, "do you really not miss any of it? The success, the money, the excitement? Don't you ever wish you had stayed on the path we were on?"

Raj smiled, but it wasn't the smug smile of someone who thought they had figured it all out. It was the calm, knowing smile of someone who had asked those very questions themselves. "I used to," he admitted, taking a sip of his plain black coffee. "At first, I missed it all—the adrenaline, the drive, the feeling of winning. But after a while, I realized I wasn't missing the things themselves. I was missing the feeling of being enough without them."

Aryan frowned, confused. "What do you mean? You don't think success matters?"

"It's not that," Raj explained patiently. "Success is important. Achieving things, striving for more—that's all good. But when your entire sense of self is tied to those achievements, it's like chasing an illusion. You'll always want more. No matter what you achieve, it's never enough because you've made your happiness dependent on external things."

Aryan scoffed lightly, leaning back in his chair. "So what? I'm supposed to just stop wanting more? Give up my Ferrari and my lifestyle?"

Raj chuckled softly. "No, I'm not saying that. You don't have to give up anything. It's about shifting your mindset. You can still enjoy your Ferrari, your lifestyle, your success. But don't let those things define who you are. They're a part of your life, not your entire life. There's a difference."

Aryan looked away, staring out of the window as he mulled over Raj's words. They were unsettling because, deep down, they struck a chord. For years, Aryan had defined himself by his success. His wealth, his cars, his power—they were all badges of honor. But now, for the first time, he wondered if that definition was incomplete.

"So, are you happy now?" Aryan asked quietly, almost as if he wasn't sure he wanted to hear the answer.

"I'm at peace," Raj said simply. "And that's better than any fleeting happiness I ever felt from chasing success. I still work. I still achieve things. But now, I do it because I want to, not because I need to. That's the difference."

The words lingered in the air between them, heavy with meaning. Aryan had always believed that peace and ambition were opposites, that to achieve one, you had to sacrifice the other. But here was Raj, living proof that perhaps, just perhaps, he had been wrong. Maybe there was a way to have both—to succeed, but on his own terms, without letting it consume him.

The conversation continued, but Aryan was no longer fully present. His mind was racing, turning over Raj's words, trying to reconcile them with the life he had built. He wasn't ready to let go of his ambition, his drive, his love for the material world. But for the first time, he wondered if there was more to life than the relentless pursuit of success.

As Aryan drove home that evening in his Ferrari, the familiar roar of the engine beneath him, he couldn't shake the feeling that something had shifted. Raj had planted a seed of doubt in his mind—a tiny crack in the foundation of everything Aryan had believed about success and happiness.

The road stretched out before him, as smooth and fast as ever. But now, for the first time, Aryan wondered if he was heading in the right direction.

Chapter 3

The Allure of Simplicity

"Embracing a life stripped of excess reveals unexpected clarity and peace in the simplicity once overlooked."

The rhythmic hum of Aryan Kapoor's Ferrari still echoed in his mind as he stepped into the quiet confines of his penthouse. His gaze drifted over the sleek marble floors, the abstract art pieces adorning the walls, and the panoramic view of the bustling city beyond the floor-to-ceiling windows. Normally, Aryan would feel a rush of satisfaction in this space—a reminder of how far he'd come. But tonight, after his conversation with Raj, that familiar pride felt curiously absent.

There was something disorientating about it, something unsettling. Could Raj really be right? Could simplicity actually hold more meaning than all of this?

Aryan kicked off his Italian leather shoes, his steps soft against the floor as he wandered into the living room, his mind in overdrive. He poured himself a glass of water, staring out at the glittering lights of the city. From this vantage point, the world looked like a jewel, shimmering and endless—a world he had mastered. Yet, beneath the surface, there was a nagging emptiness, a sense of something unfinished.

Raj's words played on a loop in his mind: *"You don't have to give up anything. Just don't let it define you."*

He had laughed it off at the café, dismissing it as a passing thought, but now, standing alone in his perfectly curated life, Aryan wasn't so sure. He set the glass down and rubbed his temples. The idea of letting go—even a little—felt almost absurd. Everything he had achieved, all the hours, all the sacrifices, had been for this. But if Raj could walk away from it all and find peace, was it really so crazy to imagine that maybe, just maybe, there was something more?

That night, Aryan lay awake, staring at the ceiling. His mind refused to quiet, bouncing between thoughts of his empire and the possibility of stepping back. But what would that even look like? The thought felt foreign, even foolish. Yet the seed of doubt had been planted, and it wasn't going away.

The next morning, Aryan decided he had to know for himself. He had to feel it. He wasn't ready to give up his lifestyle – he couldn't. But maybe, just maybe, he could experiment. See what Raj was talking about.

The first step was small, almost laughably so. He left his Ferrari keys on the counter and decided to walk instead of driving. The city streets were familiar, but in the early morning quiet, without the rush of engines or the blur of meetings, they felt different. He passed by a park he had driven by a thousand times, never once thinking to stop. But today, something drew him in.

The park was alive with early risers—joggers, dog walkers, couples sitting on benches. The air was crisp, tinged with the fresh scent of dew. Aryan found a bench near a fountain and sat, taking in the scene. The sound of water trickling from the fountain was soothing, the chatter of birds in the trees oddly comforting. It was a stark contrast to the high-octane life he was used to, but it didn't feel wrong. If anything, it felt like he was seeing something he had been missing all along.

As he sat there, watching the world wake up around him, Aryan felt something he hadn't felt in years—calm. There was no deal to close, no client to impress, no need to be anywhere but here. It was both unsettling and liberating.

He stayed longer than he had planned, reluctant to shatter the enchanting stillness that enveloped him. The warm sun on the horizon, casting a soft golden light that danced through the trees, creating a picturesque scene that seemed to pause time itself. The gentle rustle of leaves whispered secrets of tranquility, and Aryan found solace in simply being. The chirping of birds provided a natural symphony that harmonized with the rhythmic beating of his heart. In this peaceful cocoon, he lost track of time, savoring the simple pleasure of the moment.

Eventually, though, the world tugged at him, a subtle reminder of the responsibilities that awaited him beyond this sanctuary. Notifications buzzed on his phone, emails piled up, and the relentless demands of corporate life loomed in the background like an unsung chorus. He had calls to make, meetings to attend, deadlines to meet—but as he reluctantly opened his eyes to the reality that beckoned him, he felt a profound shift within.

For the first time in what felt like an eternity, Aryan realized the day didn't feel as rushed, as frantic. The usual weight of urgency that had pressed down on him like a heavy cloak seemed to lighten, lifting his spirits as if a burden had been released. It was a revelation that sparked curiosity within him. Had he really been living in such a state of perpetual motion, always chasing the next big deal or the next moment of validation? The very thought made him pause.

Aryan had always been the embodiment of ambition, a master of time management and productivity. But now, he wasn't chasing time; instead, time felt as though it had paused just for him. It was a liberating realization that began to reshape his understanding of success. He could breathe in the beauty of his surroundings without feeling the tug of the clock, the unrelenting pressure to maximize every second.

He glanced at his watch, expecting to see the familiar panic-inducing numbers, but instead, the hands seemed to move in slow motion, as if they too were entranced by the moment. Aryan's heart swelled with an unfamiliar sense of peace. He had been so focused on achieving external milestones that he had forgotten the joy of simply being. This wasn't about neglecting his duties or abandoning his ambitions; it was about recognizing the value of pausing, reflecting, and truly appreciating the present. As he finally rose to leave, Aryan felt a renewed sense of purpose—an understanding that he could blend his relentless drive with moments of stillness. He walked back to his Ferrari with a spring in his step, feeling as though he were embarking on a different kind of journey. No longer was he merely a man chasing success; he was becoming a man who understood the importance of savoring every moment along the way.

In that moment, he made a conscious decision to carry this newfound perspective with him. He would approach his responsibilities with a sense of calm, allowing space for thought and creativity rather than rushing headlong into the day's tasks. The shift in his mindset felt revolutionary. He could be a leader who balanced ambition with mindfulness, achieving goals while still honoring the present.

Driving away from that peaceful oasis, Aryan carried a quiet determination within him. He would not let the demands of the world dictate his pace. He would take control of his narrative, allowing himself to pause and relish the beauty of life. In that quiet moment of clarity, he embraced a powerful truth: the path to fulfillment was not solely defined by what he achieved, but by how deeply he connected with the moments that defined his journey.

And as the road unfurled before him, he felt invigorated, ready to embrace each day with a renewed spirit—one that honored both his ambition and the exquisite simplicity of being present in the here and now.

Over the next few days, Aryan continued his quiet experiment. He cleared his schedule of unnecessary meetings, delegated more than usual, and stopped checking his phone obsessively. The world didn't fall apart. His business didn't crumble. If anything, it ran smoother, as if the pace of his absence allowed things to breathe.

The real test came when he looked around his apartment—his sanctuary of success. The luxury, the abundance, the sheer volume of things that had once defined his status. He walked through each room slowly, running his hand over the expensive leather couch, the custom-made dining table, the designer wardrobe that overflowed with clothes he barely wore. All these things, these markers of achievement—had they truly brought him happiness?

The next morning, Aryan opened his closet and reached for the simplest outfit he could find: a pair of jeans and a plain t-shirt. He left his watch behind, the one that cost more than some people's annual salary, and walked out the door. It felt strange, almost wrong, like he was leaving a part of himself behind. But as he stepped into the world, free of the usual armor of luxury, something remarkable happened—he felt lighter.

For lunch, instead of a high-end restaurant where the waiters knew his name, Aryan went to a small café. He ordered a simple meal—nothing fancy, just a sandwich and a cup of coffee. The taste of the food was unremarkable, but the act of sitting there, alone, with no expectations, no need to prove anything to anyone, was unexpectedly refreshing.

The hours passed slowly, but Aryan found that he didn't mind. He had nowhere to be, no one to impress. For once, it wasn't about status or success—it was just about being.

Later that evening, Aryan returned home, but instead of immediately checking emails or going over reports, he sat by the window and watched the city lights flicker to life. There was something soothing about the quiet rhythm of the world outside, a world that kept turning regardless of whether he was chasing it or not.

Each day, Aryan found himself stripping away more—small luxuries that no longer held the same allure. His mornings became simpler, his time more deliberate. The noise of his former life—the constant drive for more, the endless pursuit of success—began to fade, replaced by moments of stillness.

But with each step toward simplicity, there were moments of doubt. Was he really finding clarity, or was he losing his edge? Would this experiment weaken him, make him less of the man he had worked so hard to become? Those thoughts gnawed at him in the quiet moments, but he pushed them aside, determined to see it through.

One evening, as Aryan sat on his terrace, watching the sunset, he felt a strange sense of peace settle over him. It wasn't the adrenaline-fueled high of closing a major deal, nor the fleeting joy of buying something new. It was different—quieter, but somehow more profound.

He thought of Raj and their conversation. Maybe this was what Raj had found—the ability to let go, to live without the need for constant validation from the outside world. Aryan wasn't sure if he was there yet, but he was beginning to understand. Success, after all, wasn't just about what he had—it was about how he lived.

As the city lights twinkled in the distance, Aryan felt a shift within himself. He wasn't giving up his world, but he was learning how to live in it differently. The allure of simplicity had shown him that perhaps there was more to life than the relentless chase for more.

For the first time, Aryan Kapoor wasn't running. He was just being. And in that stillness, he found a clarity he had never expected.

Chapter 4

Seeking Answers in the Corporate World

"When success intertwines with mindfulness, questions arise about balancing material achievements with spiritual fulfillment."

Aryan Kapoor stepped out of his sleek Ferrari, the glossy finish of the vehicle reflecting the early morning sunlight. The prestigious corporate conference he was about to attend was held in an architectural marvel—an imposing structure of glass and steel that stood as a testament to the very world Aryan had thrived in for years. As he walked through the grand entrance, the sense of grandeur was unmistakable, from the glittering chandeliers to the high-tech displays announcing the event.

Aryan had always been at ease amidst the opulence of corporate success, but today was different. His recent experiences—a taste of simplicity and the haunting reflections from his conversation with Raj—had left him feeling that there was something more, something beyond the conventional markers of achievement. He was here to find out if he could bridge the gap between the material world he cherished and the spiritual peace he yearned for.

The auditorium was buzzing with excitement. As Aryan took his seat, he glanced around at the sea of sharp suits and polished shoes, each person a symbol of success in their own right. The stage was set for a series of talks and panels featuring some of the most influential leaders and thinkers from around the globe. Aryan's heart raced with anticipation; he was eager to discover if these successful individuals had found a way to balance their material achievements with a sense of inner peace.

The keynote speaker took the stage, commanding the audience's attention with a presence that was both powerful and serene. This was no ordinary business leader; they were known for their remarkable ability to integrate mindfulness with high-octane success. Aryan watched intently as the speaker began their address, their voice resonating with a calm authority.

"Success is not merely the attainment of wealth or accolades," the speaker began, "but the alignment of your actions with your core values and sense of purpose. True fulfillment arises not from the external achievements alone but from the internal harmony you cultivate while pursuing them."

Aryan's eyes narrowed as he absorbed the speaker's words. The idea of aligning one's achievements with personal values and inner peace was intriguing, especially given his recent foray into the world of minimalism. It seemed like a perfect synthesis of the material and the spiritual—a bridge between his current reality and the simplicity he had briefly explored.

As the day unfolded, Aryan attended various sessions and workshops. One session, in particular, captivated him. The speaker, a renowned entrepreneur, shared his journey of achieving not only financial success but also a profound sense of balance and well-being. The entrepreneur's story was one of transformation—from a high-stakes career that left him feeling empty to a balanced life where he had integrated mindfulness practices into his daily routine.

The entrepreneur spoke of his early career days—relentless ambition, late nights, and an unyielding drive for success. Yet, despite the accolades and financial rewards, he felt a pervasive sense of dissatisfaction. It wasn't until he embraced mindfulness practices, such as daily meditation and purposeful reflection, that he found a deeper sense of fulfillment. The key, he explained, was not to abandon his high-powered career but to infuse it with mindfulness, thereby transforming his approach to success.

Aryan found himself on the edge of his seat, captivated by the entrepreneur's revelation. It was a concept that resonated deeply with him. Here was a practical application of the mindfulness he had tasted during his brief experiment with simplicity – a way to maintain his ambitious lifestyle while integrating a sense of inner peace.

During a networking break, Aryan found himself in a conversation with other attendees who had been inspired by the day's talks. One particular discussion stood out—a dialogue with a senior executive who had successfully implemented mindfulness practices within their company. They spoke of creating a work culture that valued both productivity and personal well-being. Techniques like mindful leadership, stress management, and fostering a supportive environment had become central to their corporate philosophy.

The executive's insights were both practical and profound. Aryan could see how such practices could revolutionize his own approach to leadership. He envisioned transforming his company's culture, integrating mindfulness into daily operations, and creating a work environment where success and well-being went hand in hand.

As the conference drew to a close, Aryan walked out of the grand auditorium, his mind abuzz with new ideas. The insights he had gained were not mere theories but actionable strategies that he could implement in his own life and business. The conference had offered him a glimpse into a world where material success and mindfulness were not mutually exclusive but could be harmonized in ways that enriched both.

As the conference drew to a close, Aryan walked out of the grand auditorium, his mind abuzz with new ideas that felt electric, almost tangible. The echoes of engaging discussions still resonated in his ears.

The insights he had gained were not mere theories but actionable strategies, tangible tools he could weave into the fabric of his own life and business. As he moved through the sleek corridors lined with vibrant art and plush seating, Aryan felt an exhilaration he hadn't experienced in years. The atmosphere buzzed with a palpable excitement, and he could almost taste the possibilities swirling around him like the fragrant coffee wafting from the nearby café.

He paused for a moment, reflecting on the powerful stories of transformation delivered by a renowned thought leader in the conference, illustrating how embracing a mindful approach had not only enhanced their personal well-being but had also fueled their professional triumphs. It was as if a light bulb had flickered to life in his mind, illuminating pathways he had previously overlooked.

The conference had offered him a glimpse into a world where these two realms - material success and mindfulness, were not mutually exclusive but could be harmonized in ways that enriched both.

With each step toward the exit, Aryan's heart raced with anticipation. Could he become a pioneer in melding business acumen with spiritual insight? The thought thrilled him.

As he stepped outside into the crisp evening air, Aryan felt a wave of clarity wash over him. The sky was painted with hues of orange and purple, a stunning backdrop that mirrored the colorful possibilities unfolding in his mind. The world felt alive with opportunity, and Aryan was determined to seize it.

He pulled out his phone and began to jot down notes— key takeaways from the conference that he wanted to explore further, and strategies he could implement immediately. Each bullet point became a beacon, guiding him toward a future where success was redefined.

Driving home in his Ferrari, Aryan reflected on the day's experiences. The city lights flashed by in a blur, mirroring the whirlwind of thoughts in his mind. The journey he had embarked on was becoming clearer. - **The fusion of success and mindfulness was no longer just an abstract concept; it was a tangible possibility.**

Chapter 5

Success as a Spiritual Practice

"To master the world, one must first master oneself."

Aryan Kapoor stood at the crossroads of an intriguing realization: inner peace could indeed coexist with his cherished wealth. The idea was unconventional, but Aryan was resolute. Determined to achieve spiritual fulfillment without relinquishing his material success, he set out to chart a path less explored. Instead of retreating to a monastery or seeking advice from distant spiritual guides, Aryan chose to turn to those who had harmoniously blended ambition with mindfulness. He was convinced that wisdom could be gleaned from the very realm where he excelled—among the vanguards of industry who had successfully melded success with spiritual insight.

The Quest for Harmonious Wisdom

Aryan's journey began with a series of consultations with influential leaders who had redefined success. His first mentor, Rajiv Mehta, was a tech magnate whose office exuded tranquility amidst the frenetic pace of Silicon Valley. The space was meticulously organized, adorned with calming elements like a Zen garden and soft, ambient lighting. It was a stark contrast to the usual high-octane environment of the tech industry.

Rajiv greeted Aryan with a serene composure, a reflection of his balanced approach to life. **"Our work is our meditation,"** he said, as they sat in his minimalist office with the city's skyline stretching out behind them. **"Success isn't just about achieving goals; it's about how we engage with our work. When we approach our tasks with mindfulness, we turn them into a spiritual practice."**

The concept was revolutionary to Aryan. He had always viewed success as a series of victories and milestones, but Rajiv's perspective suggested that the journey itself could be a spiritual endeavor. The notion that work could be transformed into a form of meditation was both challenging and compelling. Could he, too, infuse his relentless pursuit of success with a sense of purpose and mindfulness?

The Art of Mindful Leadership

Intrigued by Rajiv's insights, Aryan sought out additional leaders who had integrated spirituality into their professional lives. His next mentor, Maya Singh, was a renowned businesswoman celebrated for her balanced approach to leadership. Maya's office was a reflection of her philosophy—a harmonious blend of elegance and tranquility, complete with soft music and a view of a serene garden.

Maya's wisdom resonated deeply with Aryan. "In the fast-paced world of business, it's easy to get swept away by chaos," she explained during their meeting. **"The key is to treat every interaction and decision as an opportunity to practice mindfulness. It's not about escaping the pressure but embracing it with a calm and focused mind."**

Aryan found Maya's advice both practical and profound. It presented a new perspective on how he could approach his daily tasks—not as mere transactions but as opportunities for mindfulness and growth. He realized that by applying a heightened sense of awareness to his business practices, he could transform his work into a form of spiritual practice.

Transforming the Daily Grind

Inspired by his mentors and their profound teachings, Aryan embarked on a mission to redesign his office space, transforming it from a bustling center of material wealth into a serene sanctuary of calm and focus.

Aryan envisioned a space that nurtured creativity and clarity rather than competition and chaos. The walls, once lined with plaques and awards that celebrated individual achievements, were reimagined. Instead of accolades, they now featured a curated selection of artwork designed to inspire reflection and evoke a sense of tranquility amidst the whirlwind of meetings and negotiations.

In the corner of his desk, a small Zen garden became a daily ritual. Aryan meticulously raked the sand into calming patterns. This simple act reminded him of the words of Lao Tzu: "Nature does not hurry, yet everything is accomplished." The garden served as a tangible manifestation of his commitment to mindfulness, inviting moments of reflection and grounding him in the present.

Aryan's approach to his interactions with colleagues and clients began to evolve in tandem with his physical environment. Meetings, which had once been focused solely on outcomes and efficiency, transformed into opportunities for meaningful connections. He embraced the philosophy of Simon Sinek, who said, "People don't buy what you do; they buy why you do it." Aryan sought to cultivate an atmosphere where people felt valued and understood, encouraging open dialogue and fostering a sense of community.

Listening became his superpower. He approached conversations with intent, fully engaging with his colleagues, allowing them to express their thoughts without interruption. He discovered that the art of listening not only deepened relationships but also opened doors to new ideas and perspectives. When his team felt heard, they were more willing to contribute, fostering an environment of collaboration and innovation. The simple act of giving someone his undivided attention became a catalyst for trust and respect, creating a ripple effect throughout the organization.

Every decision Aryan made was now approached with mindfulness. Instead of rushing through processes, he took the time to consider the implications of his choices, weighing both short-term gains and long-term impacts. He remembered the words of Viktor Frankl: "Between stimulus and response, there is a space. In that space is our power to choose our response." This newfound clarity allowed Aryan to navigate challenges with grace and foresight, resulting in decisions that resonated deeply with his values and vision.

The impact of this shift in perspective began to yield remarkable results. Colleagues responded with increased trust and respect, as they felt empowered and inspired in their roles. Aryan's decisions became more intuitive and effective, guided by a blend of analytical thinking and emotional intelligence. The once-frantic atmosphere of the office evolved into one where creativity flourished, ideas blossomed, and collaboration thrived.

As he walked through his transformed office, Aryan felt a profound sense of fulfillment. Each element, from the artwork on the walls to the Zen garden on his desk, served as a reminder of the journey he had undertaken. The daily grind was no longer a mere obligation; it was a canvas on which he could paint a new vision of success—one that harmonized ambition with mindfulness, material wealth with inner peace.

In this new paradigm, Aryan found not just success but a purpose that transcended traditional metrics. He was no longer chasing achievements; he was cultivating a legacy of well-being, connection, and inspiration. The office had become a reflection of his evolution, a space that not only celebrated his journey but also invited others to embark on their own transformative paths. As he embraced this new way of working and leading, Aryan knew he was well on his way to redefining success—not just for himself, but for all those who crossed his path.

Rituals of Success

As Aryan continued to embrace this new approach, he began to perceive his work not merely as a series of tasks but as a tapestry of spiritual rituals, each thread woven with intention and mindfulness.

Each task, from the mundane to the monumental, was approached with a sense of purpose and mindfulness. Every aspect of his day became an opportunity to practice presence, turning the act of working into a sacred ceremony. Whether it was drafting a proposal, leading a team meeting, or simply answering emails, he approached each task with reverence, acknowledging that every moment held the potential for growth and connection.

The mundane acts that had once felt like burdens began to transform into rituals of success. As he settled into his chair each morning, Aryan took a moment to breathe deeply, grounding himself in the present. He reminded himself of the words of Eckhart Tolle: "Realize deeply that the present moment is all you have. Make the NOW the primary focus of your life." This simple practice shifted his perspective, allowing him to see the significance in even the smallest details of his workday.

The once-familiar sensation of racing thoughts and distractions faded into the background as he focused on the task at hand. Aryan discovered joy in the process rather than merely in the outcomes, which now became secondary. The act of creating, leading, and achieving became a form of meditation in itself. He found that when he aligned his actions with his values, his work became a source of joy rather than a means to an end. Each completed project became a testament to his commitment to authenticity and purpose.

This transformation was not without its challenges. Integrating mindfulness into a high-pressure environment required immense patience and resilience. Aryan had to continuously remind himself to stay present amidst the pressures of looming deadlines and high expectations.

Through the rituals of success, Aryan rediscovered the true essence of his work—an exploration of purpose, creativity, and connection. Each day became a canvas where he painted his aspirations, and every task morphed into a brushstroke that contributed to the masterpiece of his life. In this new paradigm, he was not just achieving goals; he was cultivating a legacy that would inspire others to embrace their own journeys with passion and intention. As he stepped into this evolved version of himself, Aryan understood that success was not merely defined by the accolades he earned but by the impact he made on the world and the lives he touched along the way.

A New Balance

Aryan's journey had led him to a new understanding of success. It was no longer a mere destination but a continuous practice of mindfulness and excellence. His material gains were no longer seen as obstacles to his spiritual growth but as opportunities to practice presence and discipline.

Reflecting on his progress, Aryan felt a renewed sense of purpose. His approach to success had evolved from a series of goals to a holistic practice of attention and discipline. The path was illuminated with the promise of continued growth and exploration.

The Road Ahead

As Aryan embraced his integrated approach to success, he experienced a deep sense of fulfillment, recognizing that his journey was far from complete. Eager to explore new dimensions of his evolving philosophy, he saw each day as an opportunity for discovery and growth. His commitment to harmonizing ambition with mindfulness transformed his perspective on success, allowing him to create a balanced and enriching life.

With renewed vigor and purpose, Aryan was ready to face the challenges and opportunities that lay ahead. The path before him was open, and he approached it with the same passion and mindfulness that had fueled his achievements. Confident in his quest for fulfillment, Aryan looked forward to exciting new horizons, knowing that this adventure was only just beginning.

Chapter 6

Rediscovering Passion

"Passion, once tied to ego, transforms into a tool for spiritual growth as compassion is integrated into ambitions."

The morning sun seeped through the gauzy curtains of Aryan Kapoor's penthouse, casting delicate patterns of light and shadow on the polished marble floor. Aryan sat at his desk, his gaze lost in the cityscape sprawled before him. The once-familiar sight of gleaming skyscrapers now seemed to echo a disquieting emptiness. The trophies, luxury pens, and framed accolades scattered across his desk stood as silent witnesses to his past achievements—testaments to a success that now felt hollow.

The conference, with its subtle emphasis on balancing material success with inner fulfillment, had left Aryan in a contemplative haze. Raj's words, combined with his own experiences in embracing simplicity, had stirred a restlessness within him. **He found himself grappling with the notion that his passion, once driven by ego and external validation, could be transformed into a force for spiritual growth and compassionate ambition.**

Determined to explore this new perspective, Aryan had converted a corner of his penthouse into a sanctuary for introspection. The room, minimalistic in its design, was adorned with a simple mat, a few candles, and a small Buddha statue—symbols of his journey into mindfulness. As he settled onto the mat, Aryan closed his eyes and focused on his breathing. The bustling noises of the city below faded into a distant murmur, replaced by the steady rhythm of his breath.

With each inhale, Aryan felt a sense of release that swept through him like a gentle wave, washing away the clutter and noise of his high-octane lifestyle. The air filled his lungs, refreshing and revitalizing, as if he were inhaling the very essence of clarity and peace. With each exhale, he surrendered a fragment of his previous self, the relentless pursuit of wealth and status that had once defined him. That world of finance and luxury, once vibrant and intoxicating, now appeared as a distant, shadowy memory—an echo of a life lived in the fast lane, marked by the relentless tick of the clock and the pressure of endless deadlines.

As he breathed deeply, Aryan began to explore a new understanding of passion. No longer was it about the adrenaline rush of closing deals or the thrill of accumulating assets; he was searching for a passion that transcended the superficial and aligned with compassion and purpose. It was a passion grounded in connection—the kind that reached out to others, that sought to uplift and inspire. He envisioned a life where his talents could serve a higher cause, where success was measured not just in numbers but in the impact he could make in the lives of those around him.

This transformative process was not merely an escape from his past; it was an awakening. Each breath became a reminder of his journey toward authenticity, as he gradually peeled away the layers of expectation and ambition that had suffocated his true self. Aryan felt a burgeoning curiosity about the world beyond materialism—a yearning to understand how to channel his energy into endeavors that fostered growth, understanding, and love. In this quiet yet powerful exploration, he discovered that true passion lay in the alignment of his actions with his values, crafting a life where compassion intertwined seamlessly with purpose.

The quiet of the meditation room enveloped Aryan like a comforting embrace, the stillness punctuated only by the gentle crackle of the candles flickering softly in their holders. The warm glow danced across the walls, casting playful shadows that mirrored the shifting thoughts within his mind. Outside, the city hummed with life, its distant sounds—honking horns, the murmur of conversation, the rhythmic pulse of bustling streets—served as a reminder of the world beyond this sanctuary. Yet, within these four walls, Aryan found solace, a sacred space where the chaos of daily life faded into the background.

In this tranquil setting, Aryan's mind wandered to his journal, a tangible reflection of his evolving self. The leather-bound book, worn at the edges and filled with his careful handwriting, had become a repository for his innermost thoughts and revelations. It was here that he had begun to articulate the shifts occurring within him—each page a testament to his introspection, each entry a stepping stone on his journey toward self-discovery. He filled the pages with reflections on his past, his successes, and the mounting realization that ambition, while a powerful motivator, needed to be harnessed for a purpose greater than mere personal gain.

He recalled the early days of his career when the chase for wealth and status had driven him relentlessly. But now, as he sat in quiet contemplation, he felt the urge to redirect those ambitions toward something more meaningful, something that resonated with his newfound understanding of success. The journal entries had become a canvas for his evolving philosophy, exploring how he could leverage his skills and resources to create a positive impact on the lives of others. Each word he penned was infused with a sense of urgency – a desire to break free from the shackles of conventional success and embrace a path that illuminated not just his life but also those around him.

Today as he wrote an entry in his journal, he began to envision success not as a ladder to climb, but as a network of connections to nurture, a tapestry woven from the threads of empathy, compassion, and service. He pondered how each business decision, every interaction, could be infused with intention, allowing him to contribute meaningfully to the community and foster genuine relationships. In those moments of reflection, Aryan understood that redefining success was not merely an intellectual exercise; it was a heartfelt commitment to living with authenticity and purpose.

The flickering candlelight seemed to echo his thoughts, reminding him that just as flames could ignite warmth and illumination, his renewed ambitions could spark positive change. He felt invigorated by the realization that he was not alone on this journey. With each entry in his journal, he was not only documenting his personal evolution but also preparing himself to be a beacon of inspiration for others, encouraging them to join him on a quest toward a richer, more fulfilling life. In this room, surrounded by tranquility, Aryan was not just redefining success; he was rewriting the narrative of his life, one reflection at a time.

Determined to test these new insights, Aryan began implementing changes in both his professional and personal life. He revamped his company's mission statement, aligning it with values that emphasized social responsibility and compassion. The transformation was not merely cosmetic; it involved a complete overhaul of how the company approached its business practices.

One of Aryan's first initiatives was to launch a corporate social responsibility program that focused on education for underprivileged children. He had always been passionate about education, and this new program was a way to channel his resources and influence into something that could truly make a difference. The program was designed to offer scholarships, mentorship, and support to young students, giving them the tools to pursue their dreams and achieve their potential.

In addition, Aryan introduced a series of workshops for his employees aimed at promoting personal development and mindfulness. These workshops featured experts who spoke about integrating success with well-being, encouraging a work environment that nurtured both professional and personal growth. The feedback from employees was overwhelmingly positive, with many expressing gratitude for the new focus on holistic development.

Aryan's personal transformation extended beyond his professional life. He began volunteering at local community centers, dedicating time to causes he was passionate about. His involvement ranged from mentoring young entrepreneurs to participating in environmental conservation projects. Each experience brought him a sense of fulfillment that he had never known before—a deep, abiding joy that was rooted in making a tangible difference.

One day, Aryan visited a rural school that had benefited from his company's scholarship program. The school's courtyard was alive with vibrant colors and the joyful noise of children at play. As Aryan walked through the school, he was greeted with smiles and cheers. The gratitude of the students and the teachers was palpable, and Aryan felt a profound connection to the community.

He spent time interacting with the students, listening to their dreams and aspirations. The stories he heard were both heartwarming and inspiring. Aryan was deeply moved by the realization that his efforts were not just a charitable gesture but a powerful means of empowering young minds to reach their full potential.

That evening, as Aryan drove back to his penthouse, the roar of his Ferrari was no longer a symbol of his success but a backdrop to his evolving sense of purpose. The luxury car, once a testament to his achievements, now seemed like a mere accessory to his journey of transformation. Aryan had come to understand that true fulfillment lay not in the accumulation of material possessions but in the positive impact he could have on the world.

Back at his penthouse, Aryan sat on the terrace, the city lights stretching out before him like a vast, twinkling sea. The skyline, which had once represented his relentless pursuit of success, now symbolized the possibilities of a new chapter in his life. The view was a canvas where he could paint a future defined not just by personal ambition but by compassion and contribution.

As Aryan gazed at the horizon, he felt a profound sense of peace. His passion had evolved from a pursuit of personal accolades to a journey of purpose and impact. He realized that true success was not about achieving more for the sake of status but about using his abilities and resources to uplift others and create meaningful change.

The road ahead was still unfolding, but Aryan was now equipped with a deeper understanding of what it meant to live a life of purpose. **He had discovered that passion, when aligned with compassion, could be a powerful force for growth and fulfillment**. The cityscape before him was a reflection of the new direction he had chosen—a blend of ambition and empathy, where success was not just about personal achievements but about making a positive impact on the world.

As Aryan looked out at the horizon, he felt ready to embrace this new chapter with an open heart and a renewed sense of purpose. The journey had transformed him, and he was eager to continue exploring the possibilities of a life defined not by material success alone but by the power of compassionate ambition.

Chapter 7

Facing the Fear of Loss

"Confronting deep-seated fears, one learns to find peace amidst the possibility of losing what was once held dear, preparing to let go."

The city skyline glistened with the first light of dawn, but inside Aryan Kapoor's penthouse, the early morning hours were marked by a stark contrast. Aryan sat on the edge of his bed, his mind a whirlwind of anxiety. The news from his assistant, Aarti, had shaken the foundations of his new, tranquil routine. The market downturn was more than just a financial blow—it was a personal upheaval, threatening to unravel the calm he had worked so hard to achieve.

His phone buzzed incessantly on the nightstand, each ping a reminder of the mounting pressure. Aryan took a deep breath and forced himself to focus. He needed to act quickly, but more importantly, he needed clarity. As he dressed, the routine felt mechanical, the luxury of his designer suits and polished shoes seeming almost inconsequential. For the first time, Aryan questioned the very fabric of his existence. Was his worth really defined by his financial success?

Arriving at the office, Aryan was met with palpable tension. The usual hum of productivity was overshadowed by pervasive anxiety. He walked through the corridors, his mind racing, trying to reconcile his newfound perspective with the reality of his situation. The once-familiar comfort of his executive suite now felt like a gilded cage, its opulence a stark contrast to the turmoil within.

In the conference room, Aryan was surrounded by his senior executives, their faces etched with concern. Charts and reports sprawled across the table, each one a testament to the gravity of the crisis. Aryan listened intently as they outlined potential strategies to mitigate the damage, but his thoughts kept drifting back to his recent revelations. The fear of loss wasn't just about financial ruin—it was a reflection of his deeper fears about identity and self-worth.

As the meeting progressed, Aryan found himself increasingly disoriented. The numbers and forecasts were abstract compared to the visceral fear he felt inside. He couldn't help but reflect on his transformation from a man driven by material success to someone seeking deeper meaning. The contrast was jarring, and he struggled to find a balance between his old self and the person he was becoming.

When the meeting ended, Aryan took a moment to step away from the chaos. He walked to his meditation room, a sanctuary that had once provided solace but now felt inadequate in the face of his escalating fears. The room, with its soft lighting and serene decor, seemed to mock him with its simplicity. Aryan sank onto the meditation cushion, his mind a storm of conflicting emotions.

He closed his eyes and focused on his breathing, trying to summon the inner calm he had once found so easily. Yet today, peace remained out of reach. Each inhale felt shallow, each exhale tinged with the weight of an invisible burden pressing down on his chest. His thoughts, far from the stillness he sought, swirled in an uneasy dance. Beneath the surface, the familiar knots of tension twisted tighter. The fear that had been simmering for months, perhaps years, now bubbled to the surface—an insidious, quiet terror that he had never fully acknowledged but could no longer ignore.

It wasn't just the thought of losing his wealth that unsettled him. It was the far more terrifying prospect of losing the identity he had so meticulously crafted over the decades. His financial empire had become more than just a business; it was an extension of himself. Every success, every accolade, every dollar earned had added another layer to the persona he had built—one of power, control, and unshakable confidence. But now, as he sat in the stillness of his room, that very success felt like a double-edged sword, cutting both ways.

The material success he had once revered, which had given him comfort, status, and admiration, now seemed to threaten the very essence of who he was.

But what would he be without it? This empire, built with grit and determination, had come to define him. The penthouse, the private jets, the investments, and the high-powered meetings—they had become symbols of his life's work, markers of his success in a world where such things were the ultimate proof of achievement. Letting go of any part of it felt like admitting defeat, like erasing a part of himself. It wasn't just about money—it was about legacy, about how he had come to see his value in the eyes of the world.

As these thoughts raced through his mind, his breathing became shallow and quick. He tried to focus again, bringing his attention back to the rhythm of his breath. But the calm was elusive, always just out of reach, like a distant horizon he couldn't quite touch. The more he tried to focus, the more his fears grew, gnawing at the edges of his carefully constructed life.

He had always believed in control—control over his business, his destiny, his success. But now, for the first time, he realized how fragile that control truly was. His financial empire had given him everything he had ever wanted, but in doing so, it had also chained him to it. And the fear of losing it was not just about financial ruin; it was about losing himself, the version of Aryan Kapoor that the world admired, respected, and envied.

What if he lost it all? Would he still matter? Would he still be the man he had spent decades becoming?

These questions gnawed at him, leaving him restless, even as the room around him remained still. The calm he had hoped for seemed like an illusion—an elusive state of mind that hovered just beyond his grasp. He opened his eyes, gazing at the flickering candle across the room, its flame swaying gently, as if mocking his inability to quiet his mind.

For the first time, he began to wonder whether the empire he had built was a fortress – or a prison.

In the quiet of the room, Aryan confronted his deepest fears. He had spent years equating success with self-worth, but now, with everything at risk, he was forced to question the validity of that equation.

He remembered his conversations with Raj, the minimalist friend whose simple life had seemed so foreign to him. Raj had spoken of finding peace beyond material achievements, and Aryan wondered if he was finally beginning to understand what that meant.

The meditation session turned into an introspective journey – Aryan visualized his achievements as mere chapters in his life story—important but not defining. The fear of loss, he realized, was less about the material aspects and more about his attachment to them. His identity had become entangled with his success, and the prospect of losing it all threatened to unravel the very core of who he was.

The meditation session, meant to bring stillness and clarity, quickly evolved into something deeper—a profound, introspective journey. Aryan sat cross-legged, eyes closed, yet his mind opened wide, as if an inner landscape he had long avoided was suddenly being revealed. He found himself visualizing his life, not in the fragments of day-to-day concerns or in the shadows of looming fears, but as a continuous, unfolding story. His achievements appeared like chapters—each one significant, but not the sum total of his existence. The towering buildings he had erected, the business empire he had built, the accolades he had collected over the years—they all passed through his mind's eye, each bearing its own weight of pride and accomplishment, but they no longer held the same dominance.

In this heightened state of introspection, a startling realization washed over him: his fear of loss wasn't rooted solely in the material things themselves, but in what those things represented. The wealth, the cars, the sprawling estates, the accolades—they were not merely possessions. They were mirrors in which he had come to see himself, reflections of a carefully constructed identity. His life, as he had known it, was an intricate web of material success intertwined with the core of his self-worth.

The deeper he sank into this meditation, the more he understood the complexity of his attachment. His achievements were no longer just milestones but symbols of who he had become in the eyes of the world. The prospect of losing any of it felt like the collapse of not just his empire, but the unraveling of his very self. He had spent years building this version of Aryan Kapoor—a man of power, prestige, and influence. But now, sitting in the quiet of his meditation room, he couldn't help but wonder: Was that all he was?

With each slow breath, another layer of this self-imposed narrative began to peel away. Aryan visualized the towering structures he had built as mere chapters, and he realized that while they were important, they were not defining. He had spent so long gripping these external markers of success, assuming they were the foundation of his identity. But now, in the stillness, it became clear that his attachment to them had been his prison. The fear of losing his wealth wasn't about the physical loss itself—it was about losing the sense of validation and significance that had become intertwined with it.

The thought shook him to his core. How had he allowed himself to become so entangled in things that, in the grand scheme of life, were impermanent? The luxury cars, the houses, the investments—all of them were fleeting. And yet, his attachment to them had grown so deep that they had come to define his sense of worth. He had been running on a treadmill of achievement, always striving for more, believing that with each new success, he was fortifying his identity. But now, as he sat there, his breath growing steadier, he saw the truth—those achievements were temporary chapters, not the whole story.

Aryan's mind wandered back to a famous quote he had once heard: *"You are not your successes, and you are not your failures."* It struck him now with a clarity that hadn't been there before. He had allowed his identity to be dictated by external validation, by material gains, and in doing so, he had lost sight of who he truly was at his core. The fear that had gripped him—the fear of losing his empire, his status, his wealth—was, in fact, the fear of losing the persona he had built. But personas, he now realized, are masks, not the essence of a person.

In that moment, Aryan felt a subtle shift, as if a great weight had been lifted, even if just slightly. He wasn't free from his attachments yet—he knew that. But this awareness, this understanding that his achievements were part of his story but not its defining feature, gave him a sense of relief. For the first time, he saw a path forward, one where he could begin to disentangle his identity from the material trappings that had come to dominate his life.

He breathed in again, slower this time, more deliberate. And with each exhale, he imagined letting go of another fragment of his old self. The Aryan who had once believed that his worth was measured in wealth, in success, in accolades, began to fade. What remained was someone more genuine, more grounded, and perhaps, more whole.

As the candle flickered in the quiet room, Aryan realized this introspective journey was just beginning. The path ahead would not be easy—there would be moments when the fear would resurface, when the grip of attachment would tighten again. But now, he had a new perspective. His life's chapters could be rewritten. Success, he understood, was not about what he owned or controlled but about how deeply he lived and how much he could give back.

The empire he had built, the wealth he had amassed—these were part of his story, but they no longer had to define him. In this moment of stillness, he found the first spark of something he had been searching for all along—freedom, not from the world, but from the chains of his own mind.

As the evening approached, Aryan decided to address his team. He needed to be transparent about the situation and share his vision for navigating the crisis. In his office, he composed himself and prepared for what would be one of the most challenging meetings of his career.

When he entered the room, his team was already assembled, their faces reflecting a mix of hope and trepidation. Aryan took a deep breath and began to speak. His voice was steady, but his words carried a weight of honesty and vulnerability. He acknowledged the severity of the situation and the potential impact on their collective efforts. Yet, he also spoke about resilience and adaptability, drawing on his own journey of transformation.

"We are facing a significant challenge," Aryan said, his gaze sweeping across the room. "But this is also an opportunity for us to redefine what success means. I've been on a journey of understanding that true fulfillment comes not from the wealth we amass but from the way we navigate the highs and lows of life. We will get through this, and we will emerge stronger."

The room fell silent, the gravity of Aryan's words settling in. There was a sense of solidarity, a collective determination to face the challenges head-on. Aryan's honesty had resonated, and for the first time in a long while, he felt a connection with his team that went beyond the superficial metrics of success.

In the days that followed, Aryan worked tirelessly alongside his team to address the crisis. He was deeply involved in decision-making and problem-solving, but he also made time for personal reflection. He continued to explore ways to integrate his newfound understanding into his life and work. The process was demanding, but it also provided him with a sense of purpose that transcended financial success.

As Aryan faced the fear of loss and navigated the complexities of the crisis, he began to see the value in embracing both the highs and lows of life. The journey was far from over, but he had started to reconcile his material ambitions with a deeper sense of purpose and compassion. The fear of losing it all had become a catalyst for growth, challenging him to redefine his attachments and find a more profound understanding of success.

With the immediate crisis behind him and a renewed perspective emerging, Aryan was ready to delve deeper into his exploration of attachment. The realization that true fulfillment lay not in material wealth but in a more balanced view of success had set the stage for a profound journey of self-discovery.

Chapter 8

Redefining Attachment

"True freedom lies not in renouncing possessions but in liberating oneself from their control."

Aryan Kapoor's journey was a tapestry woven with contradictions. He had spent his life scaling the peaks of material success, reveling in the spoils of wealth and power that came with it. Yet here he stood, at the edge of a profound transformation, where everything he had once clung to so tightly was beginning to unravel. The world around him—his vast empire, his towering success, the symbols of his achievements—was unchanged. But something deep within Aryan was shifting, a quiet tremor in the foundation of his identity.

This wasn't a rejection of wealth—far from it. Aryan didn't harbor any illusions about living a life of asceticism. But as he approached this next chapter of his life, he realized that his relationship with his possessions needed to evolve. The Ferrari, the sprawling mansion, the expensive watches—they had all played their role, fulfilling desires and validating his achievements. But the thrill they once gave him was fading.

Aryan's mind drifted to a quote he had once read by the philosopher Epictetus: *"Wealth consists not in having great possessions, but in having few wants.*" The words now resonated in a way they hadn't before.

The contradiction within him was palpable. Here was a man who had spent decades cultivating an empire, meticulously crafting an image of success and superiority. Yet now, he found himself yearning for something more enduring, something that transcended the material world he had built. Aryan wasn't ashamed of his achievements— he was proud of the life he had created. But the paradigm of success he had once subscribed to now felt incomplete, hollow even.

His mind wandered to another quote, this time from the Buddha: *"The root of suffering is attachment."* Aryan had heard it before, but now he truly understood it. His suffering—the gnawing sense of discontent despite all his success—was rooted in his attachment to the things that were meant to serve him, not define him.

Aryan took a deep breath, feeling lighter, as though a weight he hadn't even noticed had been lifted. He was still the man who had built an empire, but now, he was more than that. He was ready to embrace a new understanding of success—one rooted not in accumulation, but in alignment. With this new clarity, Aryan felt an unfamiliar excitement rise within him, not for the material world, but for the journey that lay ahead.

The Ferrari Evolution

The Ferrari sat like a jewel in Aryan's sprawling driveway, its sleek, aerodynamic form shimmering under the golden afternoon sun. For years, this car had been the embodiment of Aryan's dreams realized—a tangible reward for his relentless ambition, the crown jewel in the empire he had built. Every detail, from the throaty roar of the engine to the hand-stitched leather seats, had been a daily reminder of his success. The rush of driving it on open roads, the wind whipping through the windows as he effortlessly accelerated past the world, was not just exhilarating—it had been a symbol of everything Aryan had achieved.

But as he approached the car one crisp autumn morning, something in his perception had shifted. The gleaming machine, once the epitome of his triumphs, no longer stirred the same emotions in him. Where it had once held a near-mythic power over his sense of self-worth, now it was simply what it was: a marvel of engineering, a finely-tuned vehicle, but no longer the measure of his value as a man.

Aryan ran his hand along the cool, polished surface, feeling the familiar contours beneath his fingers. He could still appreciate the Ferrari for what it was—a masterpiece of craftsmanship, a machine that delivered an unrivaled experience on the road. But the key difference now was that the Ferrari no longer owned him. The identity he had once wrapped so tightly around this car had unraveled.

He realized that the thrill of the engine's growl, the adrenaline of high-speed drives—these were fleeting moments, joys to be savored but not clung to. He could still take pleasure in the way the world blurred as he sped down the highway, the lightness in his chest as the car surged forward. But the difference was profound: the Ferrari had ceased to be the center of his universe. It was an experience, a moment in time, not a measure of his success or his value.

As Aryan stood there, he understood something new. Life wasn't about rejecting the pleasures or rewards of success – it was about experiencing them with a new kind of freedom.

The Ferrari was no longer a symbol of who he was or needed to be. He could enjoy it, but now, it was with a lightness in his heart, a deeper joy in knowing that the car didn't define him.

In that moment, Aryan felt a sense of release. He would drive the Ferrari, feel the rush of the engine, but with each turn of the wheel, he was no longer tethered to it. It was just a car—no more, no less. And in that simplicity, he found a new kind of triumph. The Ferrari was still part of his life, but it no longer commanded his sense of identity. For the first time, Aryan could enjoy the thrill without being consumed by it. He had reclaimed not just his sense of self, but the joy of simply being present in the moment, whether behind the wheel of a luxury car or walking through life with nothing more than his thoughts.

A New Perspective

As Aryan embraced this newfound mindset, he reflected on the teachings of great thinkers like Lao Tzu, who said, "When I let go of what I am, I become what I might be." This principle had taken root within Aryan's heart. He was no longer defined by his possessions; they were tools for living, not chains to bind him. Whether he had them or not, his joy remained intact. The Ferrari might be a source of momentary pleasure, but it was no longer tied to his sense of fulfillment. The thrill was in the experience, not the ownership. Aryan's gaze, once filled with possessive pride, was now tempered with a contemplative calm. He appreciated its craftsmanship, its design, and the joy it brought him, but it no longer defined his essence.

Aryan's shift in perspective wasn't instantaneous; it was the result of a gradual, introspective journey. The Ferrari was still a symbol of his success, but it was now one part of a larger narrative. As he drove through the city's bustling streets, he no longer felt the need to flaunt his achievements. Instead, the Ferrari became a vessel for experiencing life's finer moments with a sense of peace rather than pride.

This shift in perspective extended to his mansion as well. In the past, it had stood as a towering symbol of his achievements, a monument to the life he had meticulously crafted. But now, walking through the opulent hallways, Aryan felt a different sense of connection with the space. His mansion, with its sprawling gardens, breathtaking views, and designer interiors, no longer represented the pinnacle of his success. Instead, it became a sanctuary—a place of peace, not just luxury.

The elaborate furnishings, the rare art that adorned the walls, and the state-of-the-art amenities—all of it was still beautiful, but now it felt as though these things were part of his life's tapestry, not its core essence. The mansion was a shelter, not a shrine. It provided him with comfort and beauty, but it did not define his worth. Aryan had learned to appreciate without attachment, to love without possession.

It was as if he had unlocked a new dimension of joy, one that allowed him to savor life's pleasures while staying free from their grasp.

'"The things you own end up owning you," said Chuck Palahniuk in Fight Club. Aryan knew this truth all too well. He had once lived as though his identity was intertwined with his wealth and success. Now, however, he realized that joy came from letting go. His mansion, once a symbol of status, became a space for reflection, tranquility, and calm. Each morning, as he sipped his tea overlooking the horizon, Aryan marveled at how detached he felt from the need to possess the moment. He could enjoy the breathtaking beauty of the sunrise, the serenity of his surroundings, and yet remain free from the desire to own them.

The Ritual of Gratitude

Embracing his new philosophy, Aryan developed a daily ritual that became a cornerstone of his transformation. Each morning, he would retreat to a serene corner of his home, a space thoughtfully adorned with simple, meaningful objects. It was a minimalist retreat amidst his otherwise luxurious surroundings, a deliberate choice to focus on what truly mattered.

Sitting in this space, Aryan practiced gratitude with intention. He would reflect on the blessings of his life—the relationships he cherished, the experiences that had shaped him, and the opportunities that lay ahead. This practice was not about renouncing his wealth but about acknowledging the richness of his life beyond material possessions. Each moment of reflection was an affirmation of his appreciation for life's gifts, both grand and simple.

The Joy of Non-Attachment

Aryan's journey was marked by a growing sense of joy that came from his newfound understanding of non-attachment.

The Ferrari was still a source of pleasure, but it no longer held the power to dictate his emotions or sense of self-worth. He could savor the thrill of driving it, but he did so with a sense of detachment that allowed him to experience the joy without being enslaved by it.

His mansion, too, became a place of tranquility rather than a monument to his success. Aryan's approach to his possessions evolved into one of appreciation without ownership. He enjoyed the beauty of his home and the comfort it provided, but he did not let it define him. The furnishings, the art, and the luxurious amenities were enjoyed as part of his life's journey, not as the culmination of his achievements.

The objects that once symbolized his triumphs, things that had previously tethered him to a relentless pursuit of more, now began to feel like mere reflections in the grander picture of his life.

This inner peace brought a profound sense of joy— joy in the knowledge that he could enjoy all the material pleasures of life, but they didn't define him. Whether it was the Ferrari, the mansion, or the lavish vacations, Aryan realized that his happiness no longer hinged on these things. He could indulge in them without being bound by them.

And in that freedom, Aryan found something far greater than any possession he had ever owned: he found himself.

As he continued this journey of non-attachment, Aryan's life took on a deeper, more meaningful rhythm. It wasn't about giving up the life he had worked so hard to create – it was about reimagining his relationship with it. He could still enjoy his successes, but they no longer dictated the terms of his happiness.

Aryan's mind often drifted to the words of the Buddha: "You only lose what you cling to." He had learned that the key to true freedom wasn't in renouncing his wealth or his success, but in relinquishing the need to cling to them. The joy of non-attachment wasn't about deprivation; it was about liberation. Aryan was still the same man, with the same Ferrari, the same mansion—but he was no longer owned by them. And that, he realized, was the greatest success of all.

Embracing Presence in Relationships

Aryan's evolving philosophy began to permeate every aspect of his life, extending far beyond his relationship with material success. His newfound sense of detachment and mindfulness found its way into his relationships, transforming the way he approached the people around him. Where once he might have unconsciously measured friendships and connections by their social standing, achievements, or what they could offer him in return, Aryan now saw his relationships in a new light. His friends, family, and colleagues were valued not for their status or material worth but for the connections and experiences they brought into his life. This change in mindset allowed him to see others not as participants in a race to the top, but as fellow travelers on the same journey of life, each with their own stories, struggles, and joys.

This shift in perspective allowed him to engage with others more authentically, fostering deeper connections built on mutual respect and understanding.

In his professional life, Aryan's approach transformed significantly. He continued to excel in his career, but his motivation shifted from seeking external validation to finding fulfillment in the process itself. His work became a source of joy and purpose rather than a means to an end. The sense of accomplishment he derived was rooted in the enjoyment of his daily tasks and the satisfaction of contributing to meaningful projects.

The Mantra of Freedom

Aryan's evolving understanding was captured in a mantra that became his guiding principle: ***"I can enjoy everything, but I'm not controlled by anything."*** This mantra was more than just words; it was a reflection of his internal transformation. It reminded him to embrace life's pleasures with an open heart while maintaining a sense of freedom and detachment.

As Aryan drove his Ferrari through the city's vibrant streets one evening, he felt a profound sense of calm. The car's engine, once a symbol of his ambition, now seemed like a companion on his journey of self-discovery. The Ferrari was no longer a reflection of his identity but a reminder of his ability to navigate life's pleasures with grace and freedom.

Living with Intention

Aryan's journey toward redefining attachment opened new dimensions of his life. He experienced a sense of openness and curiosity, approaching each day with a renewed perspective. The road ahead was illuminated by the principles of non-attachment and mindfulness, guiding him toward a life of balance and fulfillment.

With each passing day, Aryan's commitment to redefining his relationship with his possessions deepened. He learned that true freedom lay not in renouncing material wealth but in liberating oneself from its control. His Ferrari, his home, and his other possessions were cherished, but they no longer held the power to define his happiness or self-worth.

The Road Ahead

As Aryan looked toward the future, he felt a sense of anticipation and excitement. His journey was ongoing, and he was eager to explore new dimensions of his evolving philosophy.

The mantra he had embraced—"I can enjoy everything, but I'm not controlled by anything"—continued to resonate deeply within him. It was a reminder of the freedom he had found, a freedom that allowed him to live fully and authentically while embracing both the material and spiritual aspects of his life.

Aryan's journey of redefining attachment had opened new horizons, and he was ready to explore them with an open heart and mind. The adventure was far from over, and

Aryan was eager to see where it would lead him next. With a profound sense of fulfillment and a renewed perspective on life, he continued to navigate the path ahead, confident in the knowledge that true happiness lay not in what he had but in how he engaged with the world around him.

Chapter 9

The Practice of Gratitude

"Daily practices of gratitude shift the focus from what is lacking to what is abundant, fostering a sense of fulfilment."

The morning sun stretched its golden fingers across Aryan Kapoor's penthouse, bathing the room in a soft, warm glow. From his kitchen window, Aryan looked out over the city below, where skyscrapers rose like symbols of ambition, a testament to his journey. Yet, as he sipped his chai and watched the sunlight dance across his gleaming countertops, Aryan felt a quiet shift within him—a growing appreciation for the simple moments that filled his days.

He reached for his leather-bound journal, a gift from his recent conversations with Raj. This journal was no longer just a book; it was a vessel for his daily reflections and a symbol of his commitment to embracing gratitude. Aryan opened to a fresh page, the crisp white paper inviting his thoughts. At the top of the page, he wrote:

"Gratitude for today."

As he began to list the things he was grateful for, Aryan found himself appreciating the small, often overlooked aspects of his life. The soft hum of his coffee machine, the gentle rustling of the leaves outside his window, and the quiet companionship of his morning routine became focal points of his reflections. These were not just daily rituals; they were moments of peace and contentment that he had previously taken for granted.

Aryan recalled a story Raj had shared with him—a story that had profoundly impacted his understanding of gratitude. It was about Ravi, a humble farmer living in a village nestled among rolling hills. Despite the village facing a severe drought, Ravi, known for his kindness and generosity, continued to share what little he had with his neighbors. His small acts of kindness, despite his own struggles, were driven by a deep sense of gratitude for the simple joys in life.

One evening, a wealthy traveler visiting the village asked Ravi how he could be so content despite having so little. Ravi's response was simple yet powerful: "I am grateful for every sunrise, every drop of rain, and every person I have the chance to help. It is this gratitude that fills my heart and makes me rich."

This story resonated deeply with Aryan. It highlighted a profound truth—that gratitude was not about the quantity of what one had but about appreciating what was present. Inspired by Ravi's example, Aryan began to see his life differently. He started to notice the beauty in everyday moments—the gentle touch of a loved one's hand, the satisfaction of completing a task with his team, and the joy of a well-prepared meal.

Embracing this newfound perspective, Aryan began to incorporate gratitude into various facets of his life. He made it a point to express appreciation to his colleagues during meetings, acknowledging their hard work and dedication. This simple act of recognition fostered a more positive and cohesive work environment.

At home, Aryan developed a nightly ritual of reflecting on his day and expressing gratitude. He would sit by the window, looking out at the city lights, and write down three things he was thankful for. This practice not only provided a sense of closure for the day but also highlighted the abundance that existed, even in challenging times.

One afternoon, Aryan decided to organize a small event for his friends and family. He wanted to create an opportunity for everyone to share their experiences of gratitude. The gathering was held in a cozy, well-lit room, decorated with simple yet elegant touches. Aryan and his guests took turns sharing stories of moments that had filled them with gratitude, ranging from small acts of kindness to significant life events.

The event was a heartfelt reminder of the richness of human connection and the profound impact of gratitude. As the evening drew to a close, Aryan felt a deep sense of fulfillment.

The practice of gratitude had not only transformed his outlook on life but had also strengthened his relationships and deepened his appreciation for the simple joys that often went unnoticed.

Aryan's journey through gratitude was more than just a daily practice—it had become the very lens through which he viewed the world. Each morning, as the first light of dawn poured into his life, he greeted the day not with the weight of his past achievements or future goals but with a simple, profound thank you. This shift, from striving to receiving, brought a deep sense of peace and clarity to Aryan's life. Gratitude was no longer a fleeting emotion he summoned at will; it had woven itself into the fabric of his being, transforming the way he interacted with the world and the people around him.

As days turned into weeks, Aryan found that this profound sense of gratitude extended beyond just the material comforts and accomplishments he had amassed. It was not about thanking the universe for his Ferrari, his mansion, or the accolades that lined his walls—it was about embracing the simple, quiet moments that had previously slipped by unnoticed. The steam rising from his morning tea, the laugh of a child playing in the street, the gentle rustle of leaves in the wind—all these seemingly insignificant moments became sources of deep joy. Aryan understood now that life's real richness lay in the ability to appreciate the present, in its simplest form.

Gratitude gave Aryan more than just contentment— it infused him with a renewed sense of purpose. He no longer approached his days as a checklist of achievements to be ticked off, but as a canvas for finding beauty in the ordinary. The lesson he learned was clear: happiness was not a destination to be reached but a practice to be cultivated. Each moment, each interaction, carried the potential to fill him with joy if only he allowed himself to be fully present.

But Aryan's journey through gratitude didn't stop at his own sense of fulfillment. He began to recognize that this powerful mindset also had a profound impact on the relationships in his life. As he reflected on his connections—both with those closest to him and even casual acquaintances—he realized that his gratitude for the people around him had the power to strengthen and deepen those bonds. It wasn't just about being thankful for his success or his possessions; it was about appreciating the people who had shared in his journey, who had shaped him in ways he hadn't fully appreciated before.

With this newfound awareness, Aryan became more intentional in his interactions. Instead of rushing through conversations or taking relationships for granted, he started to slow down, to truly see and hear the people around him. He made it a point to express his appreciation—not just in grand gestures, but in the small, quiet moments that truly mattered. He found that gratitude, when expressed, had a ripple effect. His simple acknowledgment of someone's impact on his life often led to a deeper connection, a sense of mutual respect and warmth that had been missing before.

Aryan's reflections led him to a deeper understanding of the balance in his relationships. He began to explore the complexities of human connection—not in the context of transactions or expectations, but in how giving and receiving could coexist harmoniously. He realized that, just as he had learned to appreciate the present moment, he could also approach his relationships with the same sense of balance and gratitude. Relationships weren't about keeping score, nor were they about self-sacrifice or unbridled giving; they were about harmony. Gratitude allowed him to approach his connections with a sense of mutual respect and understanding.

His journey also led him to the profound realization that gratitude was the antidote to many of the challenges he had faced in his relationships. Whether it was resolving a conflict, offering forgiveness, or simply showing empathy, gratitude provided the foundation. By focusing on what he appreciated in others rather than what he found lacking, Aryan was able to nurture more fulfilling and meaningful connections.

Aryan's exploration of gratitude and relationships marked the beginning of a new chapter in his life—one where connection and appreciation went hand in hand. He started paying more attention to his closest relationships, understanding that these bonds required as much nurturing as any other aspect of his life. Whether it was with a long-time friend, a family member, or even a colleague, Aryan found that gratitude fostered a sense of balance that allowed these relationships to grow.

There were still challenges, of course. No relationship is without its ups and downs. But now, Aryan approached these moments of tension with a calmness that came from his gratitude practice. He no longer felt the need to dominate or control; instead, he listened more, sought to understand rather than to be understood, and appreciated the lessons each relationship brought into his life.

He realized that the joy of connection was far greater than the pride of being right. This shift in perspective allowed him to rebuild his bond, stronger and more authentic than ever before in his relationships.

As Aryan delved deeper into the balance of relationships, he found that his own evolution was far from complete.

Gratitude had given him a powerful tool, but it was just the beginning. His relationships, like his life, were dynamic and ever-evolving. He understood that he would need to continue to apply the lessons he had learned—finding joy in the present moment, appreciating the people in his life, and maintaining balance in his connections.

His journey, he realized, wasn't a straight path with a clear destination. It was a winding road, filled with unexpected turns and new discoveries. And as Aryan prepared to move forward, he did so with the knowledge that gratitude would continue to guide him. It was the compass by which he would navigate not only his personal fulfillment but also the complexities of his relationships.

The joy of gratitude was, in the end, the joy of connection—both to the present moment and to the people who made his life rich and meaningful. Aryan knew that his journey was far from over, but now, he was ready to embrace it with open arms, grateful for every step along the way. He became eager to delve into the complexities of relationships, exploring how gratitude and balance could contribute to a more fulfilling and connected life. His journey would continue to evolve, guided by the insights he had gained and the new perspectives he had embraced.

Chapter 10

Achieving Balance in Relationships

"True growth lies not in isolation but in the embrace of human connection and the lessons it brings."

Aryan Kapoor had always measured his life by the glittering milestones of success—his sleek mansion, luxury cars, and celebrated career. Each achievement had been a stepping stone, a testament to his drive and ambition. But lately, the shine had begun to fade. The opulence and grandeur of his possessions that once filled him with a sense of pride now felt strangely empty, like a trophy gathering dust on a forgotten shelf.

The Awakening

On a crisp autumn morning, Aryan lounged in his study, the soft glow of the sun slipping through the vast windows, casting a warm light over the room's marble floors. As he sipped his espresso, he caught his own reflection in the glass—there he was, surrounded by every symbol of success he had ever chased, yet feeling an unmistakable emptiness. The polished luxury that once fueled his ambition now seemed like an illusion, failing to fill the deeper void within. It hit him then, with startling clarity: the wealth and accolades he had tirelessly pursued weren't what he truly craved. The real richness, the kind that could offer lasting fulfillment, lay in the relationships he had often sidelined—those connections were the pathways to a deeper sense of meaning, if only he was willing to embrace them.

What he once considered secondary—his relationships—now seemed to hold the key to the deeper sense of purpose he had been searching for.

Deepening Connections

The Dinner Date

One evening, Aryan decided to surprise his wife, Meera, with an intimate dinner, something he hadn't done in far too long. Their relationship had always been a pillar of strength, but Aryan had recently come to realize how much he had taken it for granted. He planned a special evening at their favorite restaurant, the one where they had shared countless memories during the early days of their love story. The place held a sentimental value, and Aryan hoped it would evoke the same warmth and nostalgia that had once made them feel invincible.

As they arrived, the restaurant's soft, amber glow and the flicker of candlelight bathed the room in a warm, intimate ambiance. The low murmur of conversations, the clinking of glasses, and the gentle hum of music in the background created the perfect atmosphere. They settled into their corner table, a cozy spot that seemed to cocoon them from the outside world. Aryan reached for Meera's hand across the table, his eyes meeting hers with a sincerity that had been missing in recent months.

At first, their conversation flowed with ease, light and playful, as they exchanged stories about their day. But as the evening progressed, the dialogue took on a deeper, more meaningful tone. They began to reminisce about their journey together—the early years filled with dreams, the challenges they had overcome, and the little moments of joy they had shared. For the first time in what felt like forever, Aryan was fully present. His mind wasn't distracted by the pressures of work or the pursuit of success. His focus was entirely on Meera, on every word she spoke, on the subtle expressions that flickered across her face.

This wasn't just a dinner; it was a reconnection. Aryan listened with intent, something he had rarely done in recent years. He realized how much he had missed—the unspoken feelings, the small details that made Meera who she was. With every story shared and every glance exchanged, the bond between them deepened. The intimacy they had once shared, which had been buried beneath the layers of their busy lives, began to resurface.

As the night wore on, Aryan felt a profound shift. This dinner wasn't about grand gestures or elaborate plans; it was about the simple act of being present. He realized that true connection wasn't about how often you spend time together but about the quality of the time spent. It was in the listening, the understanding, and the shared moments of vulnerability.

By the time they left the restaurant, walking hand in hand into the crisp night air, Aryan knew this evening marked a turning point. The love he and Meera shared was still there, waiting to be nurtured, and he was determined to cultivate it. That night, he understood that success wasn't only measured by the achievements he could show the world—it was also found in the relationships that truly mattered.

The Family Adventure

One Sunday morning, with the hum of emails and meetings swirling around him, Aryan felt a sudden urge to break free from the usual routine. He glanced at his children, who were absorbed in their gadgets, and something stirred inside him. There had to be more to family time than hurried dinners and the occasional weekend movie. Without much thought, he blurted out, "How about we go on an adventure today?"

The excitement in his kids' eyes was instant. Plans for an impromptu trip to a nearby nature reserve began to take shape. No schedules, no timelines —just an afternoon to explore and, more importantly, reconnect.

They set off with backpacks slung over their shoulders, the kids buzzing with energy as they eagerly anticipated what the day might bring. As they reached the nature reserve, the world seemed to slow down. The city's noise faded, replaced by the gentle rustle of leaves and the occasional chirp of birds. The trail ahead, winding through the trees, beckoned them to leave behind their everyday distractions and immerse themselves in the present moment.

Aryan found himself observing his children as if seeing them for the first time. Their wide-eyed curiosity was contagious. Every rock they turned over, every tree they marveled at, felt like an adventure in itself. "Dad, look at this!" one would shout, proudly presenting a leaf or a bug, while the other explained the wonders of a hidden bird's nest they had just discovered.

In that moment, Aryan realized how much he had been missing—so much life had happened in these simple moments while he was caught up in deadlines and meetings. This wasn't just a hike; it was a rediscovery of his role as a father. With every step, he became more present, fully engaged in their conversations and their world. The stresses of work and business faded into the background.

The hike became less about the path they were walking and more about the joy they were sharing. Aryan laughed harder than he had in months, not because of anything grand, but because of the sheer delight in his children's excitement. He was learning that connection wasn't about extravagant vacations or perfectly planned outings—it was about being there, fully, in the moments that mattered most.

As they reached the top of a small hill, the view stretching out before them, Aryan felt something shift inside him. This spontaneous adventure wasn't just a break from the daily grind—it was a reminder of what truly mattered. His children didn't need grand gestures; they needed him—his attention, his presence, his love.

The day's journey, though simple, was profound. It wasn't just about walking through the woods; it was about walking alongside his kids, fully immersed in the moment. Aryan understood now that the magic of family wasn't found in the number of memories they made, but in how present he was in those moments. The laughter, the shared wonder, the quiet sense of togetherness—those were the real treasures.

As they made their way back, Aryan knew this was the kind of connection he had been seeking all along. No longer would he let the hustle of life steal away these precious moments. This family adventure had taught him that the most meaningful experiences often came when least expected, and from now on, he would be fully present to embrace them.

The Joy of Parenthood

Aryan's journey as a father took on new depth as he embraced a more active role in his children's lives. One sunny weekend, he hatched an exciting surprise: a treehouse adventure right in their backyard! This wasn't just any project; it was an opportunity for teamwork, creativity, and endless fun.

As they gathered their tools and materials, the air buzzed with anticipation. Aryan could see the spark of excitement in his children's eyes as they imagined their very own hideaway. Together, they embarked on this DIY adventure, laughing and brainstorming design ideas as they worked side by side. Each nail hammered and every plank secured became a mini-celebration, a shared triumph that brought them closer.

With every step of the construction, Aryan felt a wave of joy wash over him. It was in those moments of playful debate and giggles that he truly understood the essence of fatherhood. Parenting wasn't just about providing the latest gadgets or fancy toys; it was about creating lasting memories through meaningful experiences. And as the treehouse took shape, Aryan realized he was building more than just a structure—he was forging bonds that would stand the test of time.

Transforming Leadership

The Team-Building Exercise

At work, Aryan Kapoor was undergoing a transformation that extended beyond the confines of his success-driven career. His corner office, once a fortress of power and prestige, now felt different—a space that beckoned connection and empathy rather than authority. Aryan had spent years focusing on numbers, profits, and results, but recently, he'd come to understand that leadership wasn't just about driving outcomes. It was about inspiring others and fostering genuine connections.

Determined to take this new understanding to his team, Aryan decided to break the mold. No more standard team-building exercises or discussions about quarterly goals. This time, he wanted to strip away the professional masks everyone wore and create a space for real, human conversation.

As his team gathered for the exercise, Aryan could sense a mix of curiosity and uncertainty in the room. He kicked things off with something unexpected: vulnerability. He shared a personal story about his own struggles—how, early in his career, he had sacrificed relationships and time for the relentless pursuit of success. The exhaustion that had come with it. The feeling of something missing, even as he climbed higher on the corporate ladder.

"I've been there," Aryan said, "and I want us to have a conversation today that goes deeper than work. I want to know what you're dealing with—personally, professionally, whatever it is. Let's talk about what's really on your minds."

A heavy silence filled the room. Aryan knew it was an uncomfortable shift from their usual routine. But then, slowly, one of his team members spoke up.

Ramesh, a reliable and hard-working employee, cleared his throat. He had always been the quiet one—someone who delivered results without making waves. But today, something was different.

"I've been struggling," Ramesh admitted, his voice tinged with frustration. "I'm trying to juggle work with being there for my family, and it's wearing me down. I feel like I'm constantly choosing between my career and my kids, and it's draining me."

Aryan could feel the weight of Ramesh's words, the vulnerability in his voice. He looked around the room and saw the other team members nodding in silent agreement, their own unspoken struggles reflected in Raj's confession. In that moment, the atmosphere shifted. The conversation had gone from professional to personal, from surface-level to something deeper.

Aryan leaned forward, offering Ramesh his full attention. "Ramesh, I hear you," Aryan said, his voice steady and sincere. "You're not alone in feeling this way, and you shouldn't have to choose between your career and your family. Let's figure out how we can support you better— because this team is about more than just hitting targets. It's about making sure you're thriving in every part of your life."

It was a simple gesture, but it landed like a revelation. Ramesh's face softened in relief, and Aryan saw the power of empathy in action. It wasn't just about listening—it was about creating a space where his team felt seen and valued, not just for their work, but for who they were as people.

The conversation opened up after that. Team members who rarely spoke in meetings began to share their stories—about the pressure to perform, about mental health, about the challenge of maintaining balance. They discussed their aspirations, both inside and outside of work, and Aryan listened intently. He realized that understanding his team's personal challenges was just as important as understanding their professional goals.

What struck Aryan the most was how, in opening up, his team grew closer. Barriers that had once separated them—hierarchy, formalities, and workplace expectations—crumbled in the face of authentic connection. This wasn't just a team-building exercise. This was a shift in the very culture of his office.

By the end of the session, the room felt lighter. There was a palpable sense of unity, a shared understanding that they were in this together—not just as coworkers, but as people navigating the complexities of life. Aryan realized that his role as a leader had evolved. It wasn't about driving productivity at any cost. It was about fostering an environment where people could be their true selves, where they could express their challenges without fear, and where empathy became the driving force of success.

Aryan had always defined leadership by results, by profits and prestige. But now, he saw that true leadership meant empowering others, creating a culture where people could thrive as individuals. It was about more than the bottom line—it was about building a legacy of trust, respect, and connection. And as Aryan walked out of that room, he knew that this kind of success would last far longer than any quarterly report.

In the end, it wasn't just Ramesh who found balance that day—it was Aryan too. He had rediscovered the power of human connection, and in doing so, had redefined what success truly meant.

The Compassionate Mentor

In his role as a mentor, Aryan Kapoor found himself embracing a leadership style that prioritized empathy over efficiency, transforming the way he connected with his team.

One day, as he walked through the bustling office, he noticed Ananya, one of his junior colleagues, sitting at her desk with furrowed brows and a pen in hand that barely moved. The weight of her project was clearly pressing down on her, and Aryan recognized the all-too-familiar look of someone struggling to keep their head above water.

Instead of letting her navigate this challenge alone, Aryan felt compelled to reach out. He approached her desk and gently asked, "How's it going? Do you want to grab a coffee and talk?" Ananya hesitated, caught off guard by his genuine offer, but eventually nodded. They stepped into a cozy café just a few blocks away, where the noise of the office faded into the background.

As they settled into a quiet corner, Aryan initiated the conversation with warmth. "So, tell me what's been on your mind," he encouraged, his voice steady and inviting. Instead of launching into discussions about project deadlines or performance metrics, he created a safe space for Ananya to express herself.

At first, Ananya hesitated, unsure of how much to reveal. But as Aryan leaned in, genuinely interested, she found herself sharing her frustrations. "I just feel like I'm not good enough," she confessed, her eyes flickering with vulnerability. "No matter how hard I try, I always feel behind."

Aryan nodded, his heart heavy with empathy. "I understand how you feel. I've been there too," he admitted, recalling his own struggles early in his career. He shared personal stories of feeling like an outsider in high-stakes meetings, of grappling with self-doubt that loomed larger than any project deadline. "But I learned that it's okay to stumble," he added, his tone encouraging. "Mistakes are just part of the journey."

Their conversation deepened, veering away from the project and into Ananya's aspirations and dreams. Aryan listened intently as she shared her passion for creative problem-solving and her desire to make a meaningful impact in her role. With every word, Aryan could see the flicker of her potential ignite, a spark that had been overshadowed by fear.

As they talked, Aryan offered more than just technical guidance; he provided emotional support that Ananya hadn't realized she needed. He shared practical strategies for tackling her project, but he also encouraged her to reframe her mindset. "Think of challenges as opportunities to learn and grow, rather than obstacles," he suggested. "You have the skills; trust in yourself."

With each passing moment, Aryan watched Ananya transform. He saw her confidence blossom as she absorbed his encouragement, and he felt a sense of fulfillment wash over him, knowing he was making a difference. When they finished their coffee, Ananya stood a little taller, her eyes brighter. "Thank you for this," she said, her voice sincere. "I really needed it."

What began as a simple coffee chat turned into a powerful moment of connection. Aryan realized that true mentoring was about more than just guiding someone through their work; it was about seeing the person behind the project and nurturing their growth. As Ananya began to tackle her project with renewed energy, her contributions in team meetings became more vocal and vibrant. She started sharing her ideas openly, inspiring others to do the same.

In that moment, Aryan understood the profound impact of compassionate leadership. It wasn't about merely overseeing tasks; it was about empowering his team members to believe in themselves and supporting them through their challenges. Each story he shared, each moment of vulnerability, and every ounce of encouragement became stepping stones for Ananya and others to thrive.

As Aryan observed the changes in Ananya, he felt a sense of pride swell within him. The workplace wasn't just a place for productivity; it was a community of growth, collaboration, and mutual respect. Aryan's mentoring journey reinforced a beautiful truth: that success in leadership isn't defined solely by your achievements, but by how you uplift those around you.

With each conversation, Aryan fostered a culture where empathy and understanding flourished, transforming not just his role as a mentor, but the entire team dynamic. And as Ananya continued to shine, Aryan knew that this was just the beginning of a journey filled with meaningful connections and shared successes.

Learning Through Interactions

As Aryan's mindset transformed, so did his approach to social interactions, sparking a delightful new chapter in his life. He began to host gatherings that promised more than just the usual small talk, inviting friends and acquaintances into his home to create an atmosphere where genuine connection could thrive.

Picture this: a vibrant dinner party filled with a delightful mix of people—friends from various backgrounds, each carrying their own unique stories and perspectives. As Aryan set the table, excitement bubbled within him. The mouth-watering aroma of delicious food wafted through the air, but it was the warmth and energy of the gathering that truly set the stage for an unforgettable evening.

With a welcoming smile, Aryan encouraged open conversations right from the start. He wanted everyone to feel at ease, to share their thoughts, dreams, and even their quirky stories. Laughter erupted as anecdotes flowed, and lively debates sparked over everything from travel adventures to cultural traditions. Aryan's curiosity was alive; he leaned in, captivated by the diverse viewpoints that surrounded him.

As the night unfolded, Aryan marveled at the rich tapestry of perspectives being woven through their discussions. Each shared experience was a thread connecting them in a meaningful way, and he realized that every conversation was an opportunity for growth. The insights shared by his friends opened new windows of understanding, illuminating corners of the world he had never considered.

By the end of the evening, Aryan felt a profound sense of fulfillment. These gatherings were more than just a chance to catch up; they were transformative moments that deepened his relationships and nurtured his spirit. He had discovered the beauty of being truly present, realizing that the heart of genuine connection lies in the stories we share and the bonds we cultivate.

Aryan realized that when he opens his heart and mind to others, he creates spaces for growth, understanding, and unforgettable memories.

Embracing the Present Moment

As Aryan embraced the art of presence, it transformed his life in ways he had never imagined. Each day began with a renewed commitment to mindfulness, a deliberate choice to fully engage with whatever the moment had to offer.

In the bustling chaos of his work life, Aryan found moments of tranquility. Meetings that once felt like a blur of numbers and metrics became opportunities for genuine connection. Instead of merely going through the motions, he took the time to listen to his colleagues' ideas, valuing their contributions and insights. During brainstorming sessions, he would lean in, genuinely curious about their thoughts, creating an atmosphere where creativity flourished. With every shared idea, Aryan felt a sense of camaraderie that enriched not only his work experience but also his relationships with his team.

When he returned home in the evenings, the practice of presence blossomed even further. As Aryan walked through the door, he was greeted by the excited chatter of his children and the warm embrace of his wife, Meera. Instead of being preoccupied with the day's stresses, he made a conscious effort to engage fully with his family. Whether they were playing board games, cooking together, or simply sharing stories about their day, Aryan immersed himself in the joy of their interactions. He discovered that the laughter shared during these moments was more fulfilling than any material success he had previously chased.

Even during simple tasks, such as sipping his morning coffee or taking a walk in the neighborhood, Aryan learned to savor the present moment. He would close his eyes for a brief second, inhaling the rich aroma of his coffee, feeling the warmth of the cup in his hands, and letting the world around him melt away. Each sip became a meditation, a chance to connect with the sensations that grounded him in the now.

This newfound mindfulness extended to his friendships as well. During gatherings, Aryan practiced being fully engaged, leaning into conversations and embracing vulnerability. He learned to appreciate the beauty of silence between friends, allowing space for deeper reflections and shared experiences. Each laugh, each shared memory, became a thread that strengthened the tapestry of his connections.

Through this transformative journey, Aryan discovered that embracing the present moment opened doors to a world of fulfillment he had long overlooked. He realized that life was a collection of fleeting moments, each brimming with potential for growth and enrichment. By focusing on the here and now, he not only cultivated deeper connections with those around him but also unlocked a profound sense of joy within himself.

Each moment became an opportunity for growth and enrichment.

The Joy of Integration

As Aryan navigated through his transformative journey, he stumbled upon a profound revelation: integrating spiritual principles into the fabric of daily life was not only attainable but incredibly fulfilling. It was as if a veil had been lifted, revealing the interconnectedness of all aspects of his existence. The spiritual insights he had once perceived as abstract ideas began to take root in his everyday experiences, creating a rich tapestry of purpose and connection.

In the past, Aryan viewed his relationships as separate entities—distinct from his spiritual aspirations. However, he soon realized that these human connections were, in fact, vital components of his growth and fulfillment. Each conversation with his family, every moment spent with friends, and all interactions at work became opportunities to practice mindfulness and compassion. Imagine him sitting at the dinner table, engaging in heartfelt discussions with Meera, where they shared not just their days but also their dreams and fears. Each shared moment strengthened their bond, illustrating how relationships could flourish through genuine presence and empathy.

As Aryan embraced this new perspective, the joy and purpose he sought blossomed. He found that every interaction, no matter how small, was infused with meaning when approached with mindfulness. A simple walk in the park with his children became a cherished memory, filled with laughter, playful curiosity, and gratitude for the beauty around them. He learned to savor the little moments—like the sound of his daughter's laughter or the feel of his son's hand in his. These instances, once overlooked in his pursuit of success, became the cornerstones of his happiness.

Interestingly, his beloved Ferrari, once the pinnacle of his material success, transformed in significance as well. No longer just a status symbol, the car became a vehicle for exploration and adventure. Aryan would take his family on spontaneous drives, discovering new places together. Imagine him behind the wheel, not racing for accolades but cruising down the scenic route with the windows down, the laughter of his children echoing in the background. In these moments, he felt a deep sense of connection to his loved ones and the world around him.

His home, once a mere showcase of opulence, evolved into a sanctuary filled with warmth and love. Aryan transformed it into a space that reflected his values—a place where conversations flowed freely, and laughter rang through the halls. He often hosted gatherings, inviting friends from different walks of life to share stories and experiences. Each gathering became a celebration of diversity and connection, emphasizing that every individual had a unique contribution to the tapestry of life.

At work, Aryan's newfound spiritual awareness began to ripple through his leadership style. He fostered an environment where colleagues felt safe to express themselves, where vulnerability was embraced, and where every voice mattered. Meetings turned into collaborative discussions, fostering a culture of empathy and support. Picture Aryan facilitating a brainstorming session, encouraging everyone to share their ideas and experiences. This not only boosted creativity but also strengthened the team's bond, reminding them that they were in this journey together.

Ultimately, Aryan's life became a harmonious blend of spiritual fulfillment and human connection. His commitment to living with purpose and balance was evident in every facet of his existence. The spiritual principles he embraced weren't relegated to moments of solitude or reflection; they danced vibrantly in the everyday interactions that defined his life.

Looking Ahead

Aryan stood at the threshold of his evolving journey, the horizon of his future stretching out before him, beckoning with promise and potential. Although he recognized that his path was far from complete, he felt a newfound sense of anticipation and excitement bubbling within him. Each step he had taken toward achieving balance in his relationships had not only opened new avenues of growth but had also filled his life with a profound sense of fulfillment.

As Aryan reflected on the transformations he had undergone, he realized how pivotal his connections with others had been in shaping his understanding of both himself and the world around him. The lessons learned from Meera, his children, friends, and colleagues were like guiding stars illuminating the way forward. Each interaction had woven a thread into the rich tapestry of his life, creating a deeper understanding of what it meant to live authentically and intentionally.

Eager to embrace this unfolding journey, Aryan looked forward to exploring the intricate intersections of his personal and spiritual lives. He envisioned moments of deep conversation with Meera, where they could share their thoughts and aspirations, diving into the dreams that had yet to be fulfilled. He imagined joyful afternoons with his children, engaging in activities that sparked their curiosity and creativity, fostering a shared appreciation for life's simple pleasures. Each of these moments promised the potential for discovery—not just of the world around him, but of the deeper layers of connection and understanding within his relationships.

In his daily life, Aryan carried the wisdom gained from his experiences like a cherished map, guiding him through the complexities of human interaction. The importance of being present resonated within him, reminding him to savor each moment, whether it was a fleeting smile from a stranger or a heartfelt conversation with a friend. He found joy in small, everyday moments—sharing laughter over dinner, comforting a friend in need, or simply enjoying a quiet moment of reflection with his family. These meaningful connections had become the heartbeat of his existence, enriching his life in ways he had once overlooked.

As he ventured into the future, the road ahead appeared laden with opportunities for continued growth and fulfillment. Aryan envisioned new friendships blossoming, each one offering unique perspectives and lessons. He could already feel the excitement of embarking on adventures with his loved ones—such experiences would not only strengthen their bonds but also create a treasure trove of memories that would last a lifetime.

With an open heart and a mindful presence, Aryan stood ready to explore the next chapter of his journey. He understood that life would inevitably present challenges, but he felt equipped to navigate them with grace and resilience. The lessons learned from his relationships would serve as his compass, guiding him toward a deeper sense of purpose and joy.

Chapter 11

Deeper Connection with Family

"Strengthening relationships with family reveals that love and presence are vital elements of a meaningful spiritual journey."

The setting sun painted Aryan Kapoor's penthouse in hues of amber and gold, casting a warm glow that felt almost symbolic of his burgeoning journey toward deeper family connections. The soft light filtered through the floor-to-ceiling windows, illuminating the space with a serene warmth that contrasted sharply with the frenetic energy that had once consumed his life. Each ray seemed to whisper reminders of a simpler, more fulfilling existence, beckoning him to reflect on what truly mattered.

In the past, Aryan had been utterly consumed by the relentless pursuit of material success. The clatter of his high-powered career echoed in every corner of his life, drowning out the softer, more meaningful sounds—the laughter of children, the gentle hum of familial interactions, the warmth of love shared. Success had become his primary language, and in its pursuit, he had amassed accolades, wealth, and status, yet found himself grappling with a profound emptiness.

As the sun dipped below the horizon, casting long shadows across the polished wooden floors, Aryan felt the stirrings of a deep awakening. He began to realize that life's true richness lay not in the trophies displayed on his shelves or the numbers on his bank statements, but in the love and presence shared with those he held dear. It was a realization that struck him like a bolt of lightning, illuminating the dark corners of his heart that had long been neglected.

Since embracing daily gratitude practices, a transformative shift began to unfold within him. Each morning, he carved out moments of quiet reflection, allowing himself to appreciate the beauty surrounding him. The gentle rustle of leaves outside his window, the sweet aroma of his wife's morning coffee, the laughter of his children as they rushed to greet him—all these small joys began to illuminate his life. He found himself taking long, deep breaths, inhaling the sweetness of the present moment and exhaling the burdens of the past.

Yet, amidst this newfound awareness, a glaring absence tugged at his heart. He began to see the cracks in the connections he had taken for granted—the relationships with his family that had frayed at the edges in the chaos of his ambitions. It dawned on him that a truly fulfilling life encompassed more than accolades; it was about nurturing the connections forged with those who mattered most. His parents, siblings, and the family he had built with his wife and children were not just figures in the background of his success—they were the very foundation of his happiness.

As the days passed, Aryan found himself reflecting more deeply on these connections. He recalled cherished childhood moments spent with his siblings, the joy in his mother's laughter, and the unwavering support from his father. He could almost feel the warmth of their embraces and hear the soothing cadence of their voices, reminding him of the importance of family. The realization hit him like a tidal wave: while he had been chasing success, he had inadvertently allowed the bonds that nourished his soul to slip through his fingers.

In the quiet moments of reflection, Aryan's heart ached with a sense of longing. He envisioned family gatherings filled with laughter, where stories were shared, and memories were created. He missed the closeness he once took for granted—the spontaneous game nights, the shared meals, the simple joy of being together. It became painfully clear that success meant little if it came at the expense of meaningful relationships.

Driven by this newfound understanding, Aryan set out on a mission to rekindle those connections.

Reconnecting With the Treasure

One crisp autumn weekend afternoon, Aryan decided to take a significant step toward strengthening these familial ties. Inspired by a vision of togetherness, he meticulously planned a weekend retreat at a charming countryside villa—a serene oasis where his family could escape the clamor of city life and reconnect with one another. Nestled among rolling hills and by a tranquil lake, the villa offered an idyllic setting for reflection, bonding, and rejuvenation.

With careful attention to detail, Aryan orchestrated every aspect of the retreat to foster warmth and togetherness. He envisioned a weekend filled with shared experiences—

family cooking sessions, evening bonfires under a starlit sky, and heartfelt conversations that would nourish their spirits. He longed to fill the air with laughter, rekindling the joy of togetherness that had faded into the background of his busy life.

As his family arrived, their initial surprise at the elaborate setup quickly morphed into excitement and curiosity. Aryan welcomed each member with genuine enthusiasm, a refreshing change from the more formal interactions of the past. His mother, father, and siblings were deeply touched by the effort Aryan had invested in creating this special experience, setting the stage for an unforgettable weekend.

That evening, as the sun dipped below the horizon, casting a warm glow over the villa, Aryan gathered everyone around a large wooden dining table for a special dinner. The table was adorned with flickering candles and fresh flowers, while the delightful aroma of home-cooked dishes wafted through the air, creating an inviting atmosphere. Aryan's father, usually a man of few words, glanced around with a blend of pride and gratitude in his eyes.

As they settled into their meal, Aryan took a moment to share his thoughts. "I've been on a journey of reflection," he began, his voice steady yet filled with emotion. "Through this journey, I've come to realize how much I've missed by not fully appreciating the people I love. Tonight is about reconnecting and cherishing these moments together. I want you all to know how much you mean to me."

His heartfelt words resonated deeply, hanging in the air with sincerity and vulnerability. The room fell into a profound silence, broken only by the soft crackling of the fireplace. Aryan's mother, tears glistening in her eyes, reached out to hold his hand, while his siblings nodded in agreement, their expressions a mix of surprise and joy.

To illustrate his point, Aryan recounted a poignant experience that had shifted his perspective. "A few weeks ago, I received a frantic call from my colleague, Rahul. His uncle, a man who had always been like a second father to him, had suffered a heart attack. Rahul was devastated, torn between the overwhelming grief of possibly losing someone so integral to his life and the weight of managing his responsibilities at work. I rushed to the hospital to support him during this trying time.

"When I arrived, I found Rahul in the waiting room, his eyes red from tears. He looked lost, grappling with the uncertainty of his uncle's fate. I sat beside him, unsure of what to say, but my presence felt necessary. As we waited together, I listened to Rahul share stories about his uncle— the man who had always been there for him, celebrating every milestone and offering unwavering support.

"In that moment, as I watched Rahul's pain, I was struck by a profound realization: life is fleeting, and we often take our loved ones for granted in our pursuit of success. Here was a young man facing the possibility of losing someone he cherished deeply, and it made me acutely aware of how I had allowed my own family connections to wither in the background of my ambitions."

The family listened intently, captivated by Aryan's story. "Fortunately, Rahul's uncle pulled through, and I was grateful for that. But the experience opened my eyes to the fragility of life and the importance of nurturing our relationships while we still can. This retreat is my way of reconnecting with the treasures in my life, and I hope we can cherish these moments together."

His story resonated deeply, and the evening blossomed into an intimate gathering filled with laughter and shared memories. They reminisced about cherished moments from their past, engaged in heartfelt conversations, and offered support to one another. Aryan's sister, who had always been somewhat reserved, opened up about her recent struggles, finding solace and encouragement in her family's embrace. His father, usually quiet, shared a humorous anecdote from his youth, eliciting laughter that danced around the room.

As the retreat unfolded, Aryan and his family participated in various activities that solidified their bonds. They strolled along the lake, cooked meals together, and gathered around the bonfire, sharing dreams and aspirations. Each conversation became a thread weaving them closer together, a reminder of the love that had always been present, waiting to be nurtured. With every shared story and heartfelt laugh, he felt a sense of warmth blossoming within him, filling the void that had once seemed insurmountable. Aryan reveled in the simplicity of these moments, savoring the connections he had previously overlooked in his relentless quest for success.

One particularly memorable evening, as they huddled around the bonfire, Aryan's father pulled him aside. "I've watched you grow into a successful man," he said quietly, emotion lacing his words. "But seeing you take this time to be with us, to truly connect—it means more to me than any achievement you've accomplished."

Aryan's heart swelled with emotion. "I've learned that real success lies in the connections we build and the love we share," he replied earnestly. "I want to make sure I never lose sight of that."

By the end of the retreat, Aryan felt a profound sense of fulfillment. He had rekindled his connections with his family, and the experience had reinforced his understanding of what truly mattered in life. The villa, once just a picturesque setting, had transformed into a symbol of love and presence, defining the new direction of his journey.

Returning to the city, Aryan was determined to carry the lessons from the retreat into his daily life. He continued to prioritize family moments, seamlessly integrating them into his busy schedule. Each small act of presence deepened his appreciation for the family he cherished. The practice of gratitude had illuminated the importance of these relationships, and Aryan was committed to nurturing them with the same dedication he once reserved for his career.

Looking Ahead

The warm glow of the setting sun outside mirrored the blossoming warmth in Aryan's heart. Freed from the frantic pace of his ambitions, he felt anchored in the love of his family. This transformative realization enriched his life in ways he had never anticipated—an awakening to the understanding that true success is measured not by what we acquire, but by the love we share and the relationships we cultivate.

As Aryan reflected on the richness of his family connections, he recognized that love and presence were not merely aspects of his spiritual journey; they were its very foundation. Grateful for the chance to deepen these ties, he eagerly embraced the path ahead, confident that the love shared within his family would lead him toward a more fulfilling and meaningful life.

Aryan now stood ready to explore the next chapter of his journey.

Chapter 12

Mindfulness in the Modern World

"True mindfulness is not about escaping the world but finding peace within it, no matter where you are."

Aryan Kapoor had embarked on a remarkable journey of transformation, one that reshaped not just his perspective on wealth but also his entire approach to life. He learned to see wealth not merely as material possessions, but as the richness of experiences and connections. Amid the chaos of his bustling days, Aryan discovered the power of mindfulness – a practice that allowed him to pause, breathe, and savor the present moment.

This realization washed over him like a gentle wave: mindfulness wasn't about escaping the demands of the world but rather about finding a serene center within its constant motion. He came to understand that true peace was not a distant destination, but a state of being that he could cultivate in the midst of daily life.

With each mindful moment, Aryan felt more grounded and alive, forging deeper connections with those around him while navigating the challenges of modern existence. The journey had opened his eyes to the beauty that thrived in the balance between ambition and inner tranquility, inviting him to engage fully with both his inner world and the vibrant life around him.

The Urban Symphony

Aryan's penthouse, perched high above the bustling city, offered a breathtaking panoramic view of the metropolis sprawling beneath him. The towering skyscrapers reached for the heavens, while below, the city pulsed with its vibrant rhythm—people rushing to work, cars weaving through traffic, and the occasional blare of a horn breaking through the air. Yet, as Aryan gazed out at this dynamic urban landscape, he began to realize something profound: true mindfulness wasn't about escaping to a serene retreat; it was about finding inner calm amid the chaotic beauty of city life.

One crisp morning, he settled into his favorite chair by the window, a steaming cup of coffee cradled in his hands. The city below was a whirlwind of activity—a symphony of sounds, from the rush of footsteps on the pavement to the distant wail of sirens. For a moment, he closed his eyes, tuning in to the sensory orchestra around him. The warmth of the coffee cup felt comforting against his palms, the rhythmic hum of the city played a familiar tune in the background, and the cool breeze drifting through the open window brought a refreshing touch of nature to his urban oasis.

In that moment of stillness, Aryan experienced an epiphany: mindfulness could thrive right here, in the heart of the city's constant motion. There was no need to retreat from the bustling world around him; instead, he could embrace it. He began to see the city's noise not as a distraction but as a backdrop to his practice of presence. Each honk, chatter, and rustle became a reminder that serenity wasn't a distant goal but a state of being he could cultivate in the midst of his daily life.

The city, once overwhelming, now felt like a living canvas of opportunities, and he was the artist, painting his life with intention and presence.

The Ferrari as a Mindfulness Tool

Aryan's Ferrari, once a mere symbol of opulence, had undergone a profound transformation in his life. It was no longer just a flashy vehicle that turned heads; it had become a sanctuary for mindfulness, a space where he could connect with the present moment amidst the whirlwind of his daily responsibilities. Each drive was not just a commute; it was a unique opportunity to immerse himself fully in the experience of being alive.

One sunny afternoon, as the golden rays of the sun filtered through the city's skyline, Aryan prepared to leave for a business meeting across town. The Ferrari roared to life, its powerful engine humming a tune of vitality and strength. Instead of allowing his mind to race ahead with the myriad of thoughts about the upcoming meeting—strategies, numbers, and negotiations—Aryan made a conscious choice to transform this drive into a mindful journey.

As he settled into the luxurious leather seats, Aryan took a deep breath, feeling the air fill his lungs, grounding him in the moment. He directed his attention to the tactile sensations surrounding him: the cool, smooth texture of the steering wheel under his fingertips, the precise, fluid motion of the gear shifts, and the exhilarating responsiveness of the accelerator as he pressed down. Each sensation became a reminder of the beauty in the here and now.

Navigating the bustling city streets, Aryan found himself amidst a vibrant tapestry of life. The rhythm of traffic, the sounds of laughter from pedestrians, and the distant melodies of street musicians wove together into a rich symphony that accompanied his journey. Rather than succumbing to impatience or anxiety, he embraced the journey as a lesson in presence. Each red light transformed into a moment of reflection, an opportunity to breathe and cultivate patience. He observed the world around him—a child chasing bubbles, a couple sharing a laugh, and the aroma of street food wafting through the air—allowing these experiences to fill him with gratitude.

Every turn he took was an invitation to stay grounded, to let go of the worries that had previously plagued him. The once overwhelming urban landscape shifted in his perception, evolving from a blur of activity into a meditative experience. The hustle and bustle of the city became part of his mindfulness practice, teaching him to appreciate the moments in-between the destinations.

As Aryan approached his destination, he felt a sense of calm wash over him, his mind clear and focused. He arrived at the meeting not only feeling centered but also inspired. The commute had been more than just a drive; it had been a conscious practice of mindfulness, a transformation of the mundane into the extraordinary.

In that moment, Aryan understood that life's true richness lay not just in the grand achievements but in these small, intentional moments. Each drive in his Ferrari became a metaphor for his journey—a reminder that amidst the fast pace of life, he could always find stillness within, turning every ordinary task into an extraordinary experience. As he stepped out of the car, he carried this newfound awareness with him, ready to engage with the world and open to the beauty of every moment ahead.

Mastering High-Stakes Meetings

Aryan's professional life was a whirlwind of high-stakes meetings and intense negotiations, where every decision carried significant weight. One particularly pivotal meeting loomed on the horizon, one that could secure a major deal that would not only enhance his company's standing but also validate the countless hours of hard work he and his team had invested. As the date approached, the tension in the air grew palpable, with investors arriving in the conference room, their expressions a mix of anticipation and scrutiny. Aryan could feel the familiar knot of pressure tightening in his stomach.

With the stakes so high, Aryan knew he had to approach the situation with clarity and confidence. Remembering the mindfulness techniques he had been cultivating, he decided to take a moment for himself before diving into the fray. Stepping away from the bustling room, he found a quiet corner, closed his eyes, and took a deep breath. He felt the air fill his lungs, and with each exhale, he released the mounting tension. The soft rhythm of his breath became a steady anchor, grounding him in the present moment. He reminded himself that regardless of the outcome, he was fully capable and prepared.

Returning to the meeting, Aryan noticed the energy in the room. The investors sat around the long, polished table, their eyes sharp and inquisitive, ready to dissect every detail of his presentation. As he took his seat, he could sense the collective expectation, yet instead of feeling overwhelmed, he felt a calmness settle over him. This was not just a high-pressure negotiation; it was an opportunity for meaningful dialogue and collaboration.

As the meeting commenced, Aryan approached each question and response with a newfound clarity and composure. When an investor posed a challenging question, rather than hastily defending his position, Aryan paused, allowing himself a brief moment to reflect. He spoke with intention, articulating his thoughts with confidence and providing well-considered responses. His voice, steady and assured, cut through the tension, transforming the atmosphere from one of anxiety to constructive engagement.

With every interaction, he became increasingly aware of the present moment. The once-intimidating environment now felt dynamic and fluid. He observed not just the words being spoken but also the subtle cues—the nods of agreement, the furrowed brows of contemplation, the shifting of papers. This deeper awareness enabled him to adapt his approach on the fly, fostering a collaborative spirit rather than a combative one.

As the meeting progressed, Aryan felt a profound shift within himself. The negotiations, once perceived as a battleground, evolved into a platform for shared insights and creative solutions. His ability to maintain focus amidst the chaos allowed him to navigate complex discussions with poise, seamlessly integrating feedback and building rapport with the investors. He could sense their receptiveness, their eagerness to connect rather than just evaluate.

Finally, as the meeting drew to a close, a sense of accomplishment washed over him. The deal was not only secured; it was forged through a genuine exchange of ideas and values. Aryan felt a deep satisfaction, knowing that his commitment to mindfulness had transformed what could have been a high-stress situation into an enriching experience for everyone involved.

This encounter reinforced Aryan's belief that mindfulness could seamlessly integrate into even the most demanding circumstances. It wasn't just about finding calm in chaos; it was about fostering an environment where creativity and collaboration could flourish. He left the conference room not only with a successful outcome but also with a renewed appreciation for the power of presence.

Aryan realized that by grounding himself in the moment, he could navigate the complexities of his professional life with grace, transforming every challenge into an opportunity for growth and connection.

A Mindful Feast

Aryan discovered that the essence of mindfulness could permeate every facet of his life, even the seemingly mundane moments like mealtime. Breakfast, which had once been a hurried obligation, slowly morphed into a cherished ritual, a daily opportunity to connect with himself and the present moment. One sunny morning, as the light streamed through his kitchen window, he decided to create a meal that reflected his newfound appreciation for life's simple pleasures.

He began by selecting a vibrant array of fresh fruits and vegetables. As he stood in front of his refrigerator, each piece of produce called to him—the 'glossy red' apples, the 'bright' oranges that promised sweetness, and the 'crisp' greens that glistened with dew. The process of choosing became an act of mindfulness in itself, allowing him to connect deeply with the earth's bounty. He relished the tactile sensations of washing the produce, feeling the cool water splash against his hands, the smoothness of the fruits, and the texture of the leafy greens as he arranged them thoughtfully on his plate.

Once seated at the table, Aryan took a moment to breathe deeply, grounding himself in the experience that lay ahead. He approached his meal with a sense of reverence, focusing intently on the sensory experience of each bite. As he bit into the crispness of the apple, a burst of sweetness awakened his taste buds, invigorating him. The juiciness of the oranges followed, each segment releasing a cascade of flavor that danced on his palate. Even the fresh greens, with their subtle crunch and earthy taste, became a source of nourishment that he appreciated fully.

With each mouthful, he reflected on the journey of the food before him—the farmers who tended the crops, the sun that nourished them, and the earth that yielded such abundance. This act of gratitude transformed his mealtime into a sacred pause in his day, a moment where he could simply be present and alive.

In this mindful approach to eating, breakfast shifted from a mere refueling session to a practice of presence and appreciation. Aryan found himself savoring not just the flavors but the entire experience of nourishing his body and soul. With every bite, he felt more connected to the world around him, acknowledging the interconnectedness of all life.

As he finished his meal, Aryan realized that these mindful rituals extended far beyond the breakfast table. They were a testament to his evolving perspective—a reminder that every moment, no matter how ordinary, held the potential for profound connection and joy. And with each day, he was cultivating a deeper sense of gratitude and awareness, one meal at a time.

The Conference Challenge

A significant test of Aryan's mindfulness came during a major industry conference, where he was scheduled to deliver a keynote speech. The auditorium buzzed with anticipation, the packed crowd creating an electric atmosphere that seemed to pulse with energy. As Aryan stood backstage, he felt a surge of nervous excitement mingle with the thrill of the moment—a potent reminder of the stakes involved.

Knowing that this was a pivotal moment in his career, he leaned into his mindfulness practices to calm his racing thoughts. He closed his eyes and took deep, measured breaths, each inhale filling him with a sense of purpose and clarity. The backstage environment faded as he visualized the audience as open and receptive, their faces warm and encouraging. Rather than fixating on his anxiety, he redirected his focus toward the powerful message he was eager to share—a message crafted from his own journey and the lessons he had learned.

As the time approached, Aryan felt a wave of calm wash over him. When he stepped onto the stage, the bright lights and the sea of faces that had once felt overwhelming began to recede into the background. He centered himself in the present moment, grounding his thoughts and anchoring his spirit. The microphone felt familiar in his hand, a tool through which he could convey his insights.

With each word he spoke, confidence surged within him, and the speech flowed naturally, effortlessly. He engaged with the audience, making eye contact and feeding off their energy. As he shared his experiences—his struggles, his triumphs, and his path to mindfulness—the audience responded with nods of understanding and enthusiasm. Their expressions reflected a genuine connection, reinforcing his belief in the message he was delivering.

The applause that erupted at the end of his speech was not just a confirmation of his success; it was a testament to the power of mindfulness in transforming high-pressure situations into meaningful experiences. Aryan walked off the stage with a profound sense of accomplishment, the exhilaration of having shared his story washing over him. In that moment, he recognized that mindfulness had not only helped him overcome his anxiety but had also allowed him to connect deeply with others, turning what could have been a nerve-racking ordeal into a celebration of shared understanding and inspiration.

This experience solidified his belief that when he centered himself in the present, he could navigate even the most challenging circumstances with grace and ease. It was a powerful reminder that mindfulness was not just a personal practice; it was a bridge that connected him to others while making his present - a fulfilling experience.

A Personal Story: Maya's Struggle

One evening, Aryan decided to host a dinner party for his close friends, transforming his penthouse into a vibrant hub of laughter and connection. The air was filled with the delicious aroma of gourmet dishes, and the sound of clinking glasses harmonized with the music playing softly in the background. Among the guests was Maya, a long-time friend who had always been a source of strength and encouragement in Aryan's life. However, tonight, he sensed that something was weighing heavily on her—a recent setback in her career had left her feeling vulnerable and uncertain.

As the evening progressed, Aryan couldn't shake the feeling that Maya needed support. As the evening unfolded, Aryan found a quiet moment to engage Maya in a heartfelt conversation.

Instead of jumping in with platitudes or attempts, to solve her problems, Aryan focused on practicing deep listening. He invited her to share her thoughts and feelings, giving her the space to express herself freely.

Maya opened up about her challenges, her voice trembling slightly as she recounted her struggles and the emotional toll it had taken on her. Aryan listened intently, his gaze steady and empathetic. He offered reassuring nods and gentle prompts, allowing her to unfold her story without any interruptions or distractions. The conversation evolved into a profound exchange, rich with emotions, where both felt a sense of vulnerability and authenticity. Aryan found himself reflecting on his own journey as he listened, recognizing the weight of their shared experiences.

In that moment, Aryan realized that mindfulness in relationships went beyond mere presence; it required a genuine engagement of heart and soul.

His attentive interaction with Maya highlighted the transformative power of compassion and understanding. He saw how meaningful connections could provide solace and strength, reaffirming his belief that nurturing relationships were a significant avenue for spiritual growth and fulfillment.

The dinner party, initially envisioned as a simple gathering, became a profound reminder that in the chaos of life, it's these heartfelt connections that truly enrich our experiences.

Finding Inner Peace

Aryan's journey illuminated a profound truth: mindfulness was not an escape from the complexities of modern life, but rather a pathway to finding peace within its very fabric. Initially, he had thought of mindfulness as a serene retreat, a sanctuary where he could detach from the incessant demands of the world. However, as he delved deeper into his practice, he realized that the essence of mindfulness lay in engaging with life fully, amidst its whirlwind of activity and noise.

His Ferrari, high-stakes meetings, and daily interactions all became opportunities for practicing presence and awareness. He found joy in the simple act of listening, the sound of laughter, and the warmth of shared moments. Each experience, no matter how mundane, became a precious opportunity to practice gratitude and appreciation.

He discovered that true peace came from within, not from an external environment. The city's noise, the pressures of work, and the demands of daily life were not obstacles to mindfulness but integral parts of his practice. By embracing the chaos of modern life with a sense of calm and purpose, Aryan found a deeper sense of fulfillment and serenity.

Looking Ahead

As Aryan progressed on his journey, he embraced the invaluable lessons of mindfulness, recognizing its relevance in the fast-paced modern world. Each day unfolded a tapestry of opportunities, inviting him to weave mindfulness into every action and interaction. He understood that peace was not a far-off destination to be sought after but a state of being that could be nurtured amid life's inherent complexities.

With each experience, Aryan's perspective shifted; he realized that the hustle and bustle of everyday life could become a rich backdrop for mindfulness rather than a hindrance. Whether he was navigating the challenges of a hectic workday or savoring quiet moments with loved ones, he found that practicing presence and awareness illuminated a path toward profound fulfillment and inner serenity.

His journey served as an inspiring reminder that mindfulness is not a separate endeavor but a seamless thread woven into the fabric of modern living. By embracing life's challenges with an open heart and a calm mind, Aryan uncovered a transformative way to thrive—one that transcended the fleeting comforts of external tranquility and fostered a deep-rooted sense of peace within.

Chapter 13

Turning Inward

"Meditation provides a sanctuary, offering inner peace and calm amidst a busy lifestyle, aligning with spiritual goals."

The first light of dawn filtered through the expansive windows of Aryan Kapoor's penthouse, casting a golden glow across the sleek, modern decor that surrounded him. Outside, the city was beginning to stir. The distant hum of traffic and the soft buzz of early commuters marked the gradual intensification of a new day. Yet, inside his private sanctuary high above the world, Aryan sat still, immersed in the calm before the storm of daily life—a moment of stillness that had become more precious to him than any of the luxury surrounding him.

Aryan had developed the habit of meditation over time, and it had already shown him powerful results in his earlier stages of self-discovery. Through mindfulness, he had reconnected with his family, redefined success, and gained a fresh perspective on his life. Yet, despite these transformations, Aryan knew that the next step of his journey required something deeper. There was an elusive sense of inner stillness that still escaped him—a stillness that could harmonize the chaos of his outward life with the peace he yearned for inside. And it was through meditation that Aryan hoped to uncover this elusive element.

He understood that meditation, which had guided him so far, would be the medium through which he could uncover this missing element. It was no longer just a practice or a way to manage stress; meditation had become the key to unlocking a deeper understanding of himself and his place in the world. The same mindfulness that had grounded him during high-stakes meetings, helped him navigate relationships, and transformed his daily routines, was now calling him toward a higher purpose.

Aryan knew that through this deeper exploration of meditation, he could finally bridge the gap between his outward success and his inner peace, creating a balance that would sustain him in every facet of his life.

Journey to Inner Stillness

Aryan's meditation corner wasn't just a space—it was a masterpiece of intention, carefully crafted to offer him refuge from the whirlwind of his everyday life. Deep-blue cushions, plush and soft, provided a comforting contrast to the calm cream-colored walls. In one corner stood a small, intricately carved altar, a single candle flickering atop it next to a vase of lavender, its fresh scent mingling with the soft aroma of sandalwood that lingered in the air. A gentle fountain trickled nearby, its soothing sound weaving a melody of peace that washed over him as soon as he stepped inside. This corner wasn't merely a retreat; it was a portal to stillness in a world that never stopped moving.

Sitting down on the cushions, Aryan adjusted his posture – back straight, shoulders relaxed – and took a deep breath. As he closed his eyes, the rhythm of his breath became his focus. But within moments, his mind, wired to race from one task to the next, rebelled against the quiet. Deadlines, meetings, and an endless swirl of thoughts flooded his consciousness. It was as if his mind was a river rushing too fast for him to even catch a breath, let alone find calm.

But Aryan was resolute. He recalled something Raj, his friend, had once said during one of their long conversations. *"Meditation isn't about silencing the mind instantly,"* Raj had explained. *"It's about recognizing the noise and gently guiding it toward stillness."* With that in mind, Aryan took another breath, deeper this time. He imagined drawing in calm with every inhale, and as he exhaled, he released the tension knotted inside him. Little by little, something shifted. The storm inside his mind began to ease, replaced by a subtle, quiet calm.

Days turned into weeks, and Aryan's daily meditation sessions slowly evolved. Each morning, he peeled away another layer of the noise, uncovering pockets of peace he didn't know existed within him. Aryan's meditation practice continued to deepen as he explored new ways to connect with his inner self.

Guided Meditation

One morning, feeling the usual pull of his mind's distractions, he decided to try a guided meditation for the first time. As he settled into his familiar corner, he put on his headphones and pressed play. A soothing voice, soft and gentle like the rustling of leaves in the wind, invited him to close his eyes and imagine a path leading to a serene, hidden sanctuary.

At first, it felt strange to follow someone else's voice, but soon the words painted vivid pictures in his mind. The path appeared before him—a winding trail through a dense, misty forest. He could hear the distant chirping of birds and the soft crunch of leaves underfoot. As the guide's voice described the scene, Aryan felt as though he was truly walking that path, each step grounding him deeper in the present moment. The tension he carried seemed to dissolve into the rich earth beneath him.

The guided meditation continued, leading Aryan to a crystal-clear lake at the heart of the forest. The guide encouraged him to imagine the water, still and reflective, mirroring the sky above. Aryan pictured himself standing at the water's edge, its surface so calm that it felt like time itself had slowed. The voice invited him to release his worries into the lake, to let them ripple out and disappear. With each exhale, he envisioned his anxieties—work pressures, personal doubts, and the stress of daily life—floating away, sinking into the depths where they could no longer touch him.

The imagery felt so real that Aryan could almost feel the cool breeze on his face, smell the earthy scent of the forest, and hear the gentle lapping of water. The experience was transformative; it wasn't just a mental exercise, but a full-body immersion into peace.

These guided sessions became an integral part of Aryan's routine, offering him a structured way to delve deeper into his practice. Each new visualization or technique felt like peeling back another layer of his stress and uncovering a reservoir of calm he hadn't known was there.

The guided meditations also allowed Aryan to explore emotions he had buried beneath his fast-paced life. There were days when the guided voice would ask him to reflect on gratitude, encouraging him to recall moments of joy, kindness, and success. Aryan found himself unexpectedly emotional, as memories of both triumphs and struggles surfaced. But instead of pushing them away, he embraced them, sitting with his feelings and letting them pass through him without judgment.

This practice of guided meditation wasn't just about finding momentary peace—it was a way for Aryan to actively reshape how he experienced his life. Each session, each image, and each breath brought him closer to an inner stillness he could carry into his everyday interactions. The chaotic noise of the city, the pressures of his high-profile career, and the demands of his relationships all began to feel less overwhelming. Instead, they became like the ripples in the lake—small disturbances on the surface of an otherwise vast, tranquil existence.

Guided meditation had unlocked a new dimension of mindfulness for Aryan, one that allowed him not just to escape into peaceful imagery but to return to his life with a deeper, more grounded sense of presence.

As Aryan continued, he could feel a deeper transformation taking place. This wasn't just about calming his mind for a few minutes each morning; it was about changing how he moved through his entire day. Meditation was no longer just a practice—it became the key to unlocking the inner stillness he craved. Every session brought him closer to balancing the chaos of his outward life with the peace he was slowly discovering within. His sanctuary wasn't merely a physical space anymore—it had become the gateway to something far more profound.

At the Retreat

Seeking deeper enrichment, Aryan embarked on a weekend retreat dedicated to mindfulness and meditation. Nestled in a picturesque location surrounded by lush forests and tranquil lakes, the retreat offered a serene escape from the relentless pace of city life. As soon as Aryan arrived, he was captivated by the profound stillness of the place. The air was crisp, the only sounds coming from the gentle rustling of leaves and the distant calls of birds—a sharp contrast to the constant noise and buzz he was used to. It was the perfect setting for introspection and transformation.

The retreat was designed to immerse participants in a variety of meditation techniques, each intended to deepen their understanding and refine their practice. Aryan welcomed the opportunity to explore these new methods, feeling both excited and a little apprehensive. He knew this was the next step in his journey—one that would take him beyond the mindfulness routines he had established and challenge him to go further inward.

Body Scan Meditation

During one of the early sessions, Aryan was introduced to body scan meditation, a technique that invited him to bring awareness to every inch of his physical being. The instructor's voice was soft yet grounding, guiding participants to direct their attention to each part of their body, starting from the tips of their toes and moving upward to the crown of their head. Aryan imagined a warm, golden light flowing through him, gradually dissolving the tension he hadn't realized he was holding. As he scanned his body, he became acutely aware of the subtle aches, tightness, and emotions that had been stored in his muscles and joints. The practice was deeply transformative, awakening a newfound sensitivity to both his physical and emotional states.

Visualization Meditation

At the retreat, Aryan had a session on visualization meditation - The instructor invited participants to close their eyes, guiding them into a state of relaxation through deep, rhythmic breathing. Aryan settled into his posture, his mind open and receptive to the experience.

The exercise began by having the group visualize a gentle, warm light at the center of their being. Aryan pictured the light as a glowing orb within his chest, faint at first but growing steadily brighter with each inhale. As he focused on his breath, the warmth of the light intensified, filling him with a comforting energy that seemed to radiate from his very core. He imagined this golden glow expanding outward, spreading through his limbs, his torso, and eventually, his entire body. The light wasn't just a visual element; it carried a sensation of healing, enveloping him in peace and serenity.

As the meditation progressed, Aryan allowed the light to grow even further. It expanded beyond his body, radiating outward into the space around him, as if he were encased in a glowing aura of warmth and protection. The visualization brought with it a profound sense of interconnectedness. He felt as though the light wasn't just his—it was a universal energy, one that flowed through him but also touched the people, the nature, and even the very air around him. In this moment, Aryan was no longer a solitary individual meditating in a room—he was part of something vast, timeless, and eternal.

This visualization practice became one of the most transformative experiences of the retreat for Aryan. It wasn't just about calming the mind; it was about feeling a deep connection to the world around him, a sense of being part of a larger whole. The warm, golden glow symbolized not only the inner peace he was cultivating but also his ability to share that peace with others. The exercise left him with a sense of lightness, as if the weight of his worldly responsibilities had temporarily melted away, replaced by this radiant, boundless energy.

Loving-kindness Meditation

Another highlight of the retreat was a session on loving-kindness meditation. Aryan was encouraged to send positive thoughts and feelings toward himself and others. As he repeated the phrases of goodwill and compassion, he felt a deep sense of connection and warmth. The exercise allowed him to extend the kindness he had cultivated inwardly to those around him, fostering a more profound sense of empathy and love.

Back from Retreat

Aryan's experiences at the retreat, particularly the body scan, loving-kindness, and visualization meditations, had a profound ripple effect on his life.

His morning meditation sessions evolved, no longer limited to mere mindfulness practices but now enriched with body scan, loving-kindness, and visualization exercises that allowed him to embrace each day with clarity and purpose. As he sat in his meditation corner back home, the gentle scent of sandalwood in the air, he would often visualize the golden light filling the room, connecting him to the tranquility he had discovered during the retreat.

Looking Ahead

The retreat had not only deepened Aryan's meditation practice but also broadened his understanding of mindfulness. It was no longer just about silencing the mind or being present in the moment. It had become a way to harness inner light, radiate compassion, and extend peace to the world around him. This realization became a cornerstone of Aryan's journey, guiding him toward a more integrated, mindful life where the boundaries between meditation and daily living blurred.

In every action, from his interactions with friends to the challenges he faced in his career, he carried that warm, golden glow with him – an ever-present reminder of the peace he had discovered within.

In sharing these practices with his loved ones, Aryan found that meditation was not just a solitary path but a communal one, where shared silence and reflection could foster deeper connections. The visualization of light, in particular, became a practice he often revisited with friends and family, inviting them to join in moments of collective peace. These sessions created a shared energy that transcended words, allowing those close to him to feel the same lightness and connection he had found.

Ultimately, Aryan realized that meditation had not only transformed him but also his relationships, his work, and his very way of being in the world. What had started as a personal retreat had blossomed into a way of life, where mindfulness, compassion, and light were woven into every moment. The golden glow was no longer confined to his meditation space—it was now a part of him, radiating outward in everything he did.

Looking ahead, Aryan knew that his journey was far from over. While he had uncovered a deep well of inner peace, he also recognized that life would continue to present new challenges, distractions, and opportunities for growth. He welcomed these with a newfound perspective, understanding that each moment—whether filled with joy or adversity—was another chance to deepen his practice. Aryan envisioned expanding his mindfulness beyond meditation sessions, applying the principles of presence, compassion, and stillness to every corner of his life. He looked forward to new experiences with excitement, no longer seeking escape from the chaos but embracing it as part of his evolving journey. The path ahead was one of continual exploration, where peace wasn't a destination but an ever-present companion.

Chapter 14

Transforming Work into a Spiritual Practice

"Integrating mindfulness into work, treating each task as a spiritual exercise, leads to achieving success without stress."

The city bustled with its usual energy as Aryan Kapoor navigated the busy streets on his way to the office. But today, there was a palpable shift in his demeanor. Gone was the harried rush that usually accompanied his morning commute. Instead, Aryan felt a sense of serene purpose, a quiet confidence that the workday ahead was not just a series of tasks but an opportunity for spiritual practice.

As he walked, the sounds of honking horns and chattering crowds faded into the background, replaced by a gentle rhythm of his own thoughts. He was no longer just a passenger in the frenetic pace of urban life; he was an active participant, breathing in the energy of the world around him while maintaining his inner calm. Each step felt deliberate, each moment an invitation to practice presence.

Aryan had spent the last few weeks immersing himself in mindfulness, drawn to its promise of peace and focus. Meditation had become a cornerstone of his routine, a sanctuary from the chaos of his high-stakes career. He envisioned it as a wellspring of clarity, fueling not only his professional endeavors but also enriching his personal relationships. As he entered his sleek, glass-walled office, he brought with him a newfound perspective: to transform his work into a spiritual practice.

The office, with its panoramic views of the sprawling cityscape and minimalist design, seemed almost like a canvas waiting to be painted with intention. Sunlight poured in, casting playful shadows on the polished floor. Aryan paused for a moment, taking in the beauty of the scene before him. He had always been proud of his accomplishments—the luxury of his office, the prestigious clients, and the high-profile projects. Yet, beneath the glittering surface lay a growing realization that success, while fulfilling, had often come at the cost of inner peace.

Now, with each task he undertook, Aryan felt empowered to infuse mindfulness into his work. He envisioned meetings not merely as transactions but as opportunities for connection and collaboration. The emails he crafted were not just communications but heartfelt exchanges. Each interaction was a chance to practice presence, to truly listen, and to engage authentically. By shifting his mindset, he transformed the ordinary into the extraordinary, allowing the essence of mindfulness to flow through every aspect of his day.

As Aryan settled into his workspace, he smiled to himself, understanding that this journey was about more than just achieving professional goals; it was about cultivating a way of being that aligned with his values. The city's chaos could still swirl around him, but he now stood anchored in a profound sense of purpose, ready to embrace whatever the day had in store.

Facing the Storm of Anxiety

On this particular day, Aryan Kapoor stood at the edge of a precipice, his heart racing in sync with the ticking clock. He was preparing for a crucial client presentation, one that held the promise of securing a significant contract for his company—a moment that could redefine his career. Yet, as he reviewed the details, a familiar knot of anxiety tightened in his chest, like a vise squeezing his thoughts. His mind buzzed incessantly, swirling with pressure, fear of failure, and the relentless weight of expectations.

Preparation – A Sacred Ritual

In the midst of this storm, a flicker of inspiration ignited in Aryan's mind, reminiscent of a story he had once read about a renowned chef named Kumar. Chef Kumar was celebrated for his exquisite culinary creations, each dish a masterpiece of flavor and artistry. But behind the glamour of his profession lay a grueling reality. During a particularly challenging phase in his career, he found solace in mindfulness. He transformed his kitchen into a sanctuary, viewing each meal preparation as a sacred ritual. He focused on the textures, flavors, and aromas, treating the act of cooking not as a chore but as a form of meditation. This practice not only elevated his culinary prowess but also infused his work with a profound sense of joy and fulfillment. Aryan had been deeply moved by Chef Kumar's journey, and as he prepared for his own presentation, that inspiration surged within him.

Drawing on Chef Kumar's approach, Aryan made a conscious decision to infuse mindfulness into his preparation.

He closed his eyes, taking a moment to center himself amidst the chaos of thoughts. With each deep breath, he imagined drawing in calmness and clarity, envisioning each inhale as a wave of serenity washing over him. With every exhale, he released the stress and tension that had been building like a pressure cooker. When he opened his eyes, he felt a renewed sense of purpose and focus, ready to embrace the moment ahead.

As the presentation commenced, Aryan approached each slide and point with deliberate attention. This was no longer just a performance; it was an opportunity to connect authentically with his audience. He shifted his focus from the need to impress to the intention of communicating clearly and meaningfully. Each word he spoke was imbued with authenticity, drawing his listeners into a shared experience rather than a mere exchange of information.

Navigating Anxiety

A pivotal moment unfolded when a client raised a challenging question, the kind that could easily send anyone spiraling into panic. Aryan felt a surge of anxiety, the familiar wave crashing over him. But instead of succumbing to it, he remembered his mindfulness practice. He took a deep breath, allowing the air to fill his lungs as he calmly acknowledged the question. In that moment of pause, he felt the weight of expectation lift, replaced by a sense of clarity. With thoughtful consideration, he crafted his response, articulating his ideas with confidence. The client's reaction was positive, and Aryan sensed a shift in the room's energy—an electric current of engagement sparked by authenticity.

The presentation ended successfully, the contract secured. But for Aryan, the true victory lay not in the tangible outcome but in how he had approached the task. He had navigated the storm of pressure with grace, turning what could have been a high-stress performance into an opportunity for genuine connection. It was a profound revelation that resonated deeply within him: success was not solely measured by results but by the quality of presence he brought to each moment.

Navigating Critical Decisions

One afternoon, as the sun cast a golden hue over his office, Aryan found himself immersed in a complex project that had consumed his attention for weeks. Charts and data sprawled across his desk, each representing countless hours of hard work and potential. However, a critical decision loomed before him, one that could significantly impact the project's outcome and the future of his company. The usual stress of making the right choice threatened to engulf him, swirling around like a tempest, filling his mind with a cacophony of doubt and anxiety.

But Aryan had learned well during his journey. This time, instead of succumbing to the pressure, he paused. He took a step back from the clutter of his desk, allowing himself the space to breathe. The air felt heavier with expectation, but Aryan embraced the moment, remembering the lessons he had absorbed from his meditation practice. He focused on his breath, inhaling deeply to center himself, and exhaling slowly to release the tension that had gathered in his shoulders.

Reflecting on Values and Vision

With his mind now clearer, Aryan began to reflect on the broader implications of his decision. He visualized the potential outcomes, considering not only the immediate impact on the project but also how it resonated with his core values. What was the purpose behind this decision? Did it align with the vision he held for his work and life? As he pondered these questions, he felt a sense of calm wash over him, guiding him toward a deeper understanding of what truly mattered.

He envisioned the consequences of each option before him, weighing the benefits against the potential drawbacks. Rather than rushing to find the quickest solution, Aryan approached the decision with curiosity and openness. He took note of his intuition—the subtle nudges that often went unnoticed amid the noise of stress.

In this reflective space, he felt empowered to consider the long-term ramifications of his choice, not just for himself but for his team and the company as a whole.

A Transformative Choice

After careful contemplation, Aryan recognized that the path leading to collaboration and shared success resonated most with his values. He decided to advocate for a decision that prioritized teamwork and inclusivity over a solitary pursuit of victory. This approach would not only enhance the project's potential but also foster a sense of unity among his colleagues, creating a culture of support and shared responsibility.

With a renewed sense of purpose, Aryan confidently presented his decision to his team, articulating the rationale behind his choice. His commitment to integrating spirituality into his professional journey was palpable, infusing the discussion with an atmosphere of respect and collaboration. As he watched his colleagues engage in the conversation, he realized that the decision had transformed into a collective effort, strengthening their bond and reinforcing the values they all shared.

In the aftermath of the decision, Aryan felt a profound sense of satisfaction. Not only had he navigated a complex situation with grace, but he had also reinforced his commitment to living a mindful life—one where spirituality and professionalism intertwined harmoniously. The experience solidified his belief that mindfulness was not merely a personal practice but a powerful tool that could influence the dynamics of his work environment.

As he returned to his desk, Aryan felt lighter, the weight of uncertainty lifted. He knew that moving forward, he would continue to apply these mindfulness principles, allowing them to guide his actions and decisions. Each challenge would become an opportunity for reflection, growth, and connection—transforming the way he approached not just his work but every aspect of his life.

A Ripple Effect - Inspiring Change in the Workplace

Aryan's transformation did not go unnoticed by his colleagues. As he strode through the bustling office, there was an undeniable shift in the air—a palpable energy that seemed to radiate from him. Colleagues exchanged glances, whispering about the calm presence that had emerged amidst the usual chaos of deadlines and demands. Gone were the frantic days of frenzied multitasking; Aryan had become a beacon of serenity, and curiosity began to bubble up among his peers.

"What's your secret, Aryan?" they asked, eyes sparkling with intrigue, as they approached him one by one. "How have you managed to turn the storm into a breeze?" With each question, Aryan felt a spark ignite within him. He recognized this as an opportunity to share not just his journey but also a revolutionary approach to work that blended ambition with inner peace. He spoke candidly about his newfound commitment to mindfulness, illuminating the path he had carved through the clutter of corporate life.

Mindfulness in Action: A Transformative Meeting

In one particularly electrifying meeting, Aryan decided to take the plunge and facilitate a discussion centered on stress management. The atmosphere was charged with anticipation; the team was curious but skeptical. Could mindfulness truly make a difference in their high-pressure environment?

Aryan began by sharing his own story, painting a vivid picture of the chaos he had once navigated. With his words, he created a connection, inviting them into his world of transformation. He could feel their attention shift as he introduced the concept of mindfulness into the conversation. "Let's do something different today," he proposed, a smile dancing on his lips. He guided them through a short mindfulness exercise, encouraging everyone to close their eyes and take a deep breath.

As they inhaled, Aryan instructed them to envision a wave of calm washing over them, soothing their racing minds. With each exhale, they released the weight of the world, letting go of their worries and stresses. The room fell silent, and an electrifying energy filled the air, as if the team were experiencing a collective awakening.

When they opened their eyes, Aryan watched as faces transformed—tension melted away, and smiles bloomed like flowers in spring. The energy shifted, and he could see it in their eyes; they had just tasted something extraordinary. The team responded enthusiastically, eager to explore mindfulness and integrate it into their daily routines.

A Testament to Balance and Fulfillment

As days turned into weeks, Aryan's journey of transforming work into a spiritual practice blossomed into a vibrant movement within the office. What began as a personal endeavor evolved into a collective quest for balance and fulfillment. Aryan's colleagues, inspired by his unwavering commitment, started embracing mindfulness as part of their work culture.

Meetings morphed into opportunities for meaningful dialogue, where ideas flowed freely, and laughter replaced stress. They created a space where every voice was valued, where the frenetic pace of deadlines transformed into a rhythm of collaboration. Aryan could feel the shift within himself and his team—a newfound sense of camaraderie that electrified the atmosphere.

During a pivotal brainstorming session, Aryan introduced gratitude journaling. "Let's take a moment to reflect on what we appreciate," he encouraged, igniting a wave of excitement. Colleagues eagerly shared their thoughts, celebrating both personal and professional victories. The room buzzed with positivity, and Aryan realized they were no longer just a team; they were a community thriving on shared purpose and mindfulness.

Continuing the Journey: Balance and Connection

Aryan's approach to work as a spiritual practice marked a thrilling evolution in his journey. Each day was a new adventure, a chance to infuse intention and mindfulness into the fabric of his professional life. The office, once a battleground of stress and competition, transformed into a sanctuary of growth and connection.

With every challenge that arose, Aryan faced it head-on, armed with the principles of mindfulness. A complex project could have once sent him spiraling into doubt, but now, he approached it with clarity and confidence. As he pondered critical decisions, he tapped into the collective energy of his team, drawing strength from their shared commitment to balance and fulfillment.

He realized that true success was not merely about personal achievement; it was about fostering a vibrant culture where everyone thrived. Aryan's heart raced with excitement as he envisioned the future—a workplace where mindfulness reigned supreme, where each individual felt empowered to bring their best selves to work.

As he moves forward, he carries the exhilarating knowledge that he is not just transforming his own life but igniting a movement that could illuminate the path for others.

His journey was no longer a solitary quest for success; it had blossomed into a vibrant tapestry woven in a manner that each day was an opportunity to embrace the present, to engage authentically with the world, and to cultivate a life where spirituality and professionalism coexisted harmoniously.

Aryan Kapoor was not just navigating the challenges of his career; he was crafting a legacy of mindful mastery that would inspire those around him to embark on their journeys of self-discovery and fulfillment.

Chapter 15

The Power of Acceptance

"Embracing imperfection and uncertainty, acceptance of mistakes becomes a key to maintaining inner peace and growth."

The early morning sun cast a soft, golden hue across Aryan Kapoor's office, bathing the sleek, modern space in a gentle glow. The floor-to-ceiling windows framed the sprawling cityscape below, where streets crisscrossed like veins through a living, breathing organism. From his high-rise vantage point, Aryan could see the intricate web of life unfolding, yet today, it all seemed distant, detached—just like him.

His office was the epitome of success: a minimalist haven of glass and chrome, punctuated by meticulously organized papers, framed accolades, and the ever-present aroma of freshly brewed coffee. Everything was in its place, except for Aryan. Despite the orderly surroundings, a storm brewed within him, threatening to dismantle the very foundation of the life he had built.

The Fall from Triumph

It wasn't just another project. It was *the* project—Aryan's masterpiece, the culmination of months of tireless work and ambition. He had poured his heart, soul, and expertise into it, certain that it would be the crowning achievement of his career. But instead of accolades and celebration, the project unraveled before his eyes. Missed deadlines, unmet client expectations, and a mounting pile of frustrations replaced the excitement and optimism that had once surrounded the venture.

Each day, Aryan found himself spiraling deeper into the chaos. Meetings turned into damage control, and his once-impeccable reputation seemed to teeter on the edge of collapse. The pressure was suffocating, like a vise tightening around his chest with every passing hour. He prided himself on being the one who could always fix things, the leader who could turn even the direst situations into success stories. But this time, his usual methods were failing him, and the weight of it all was becoming unbearable.

An Evening of Reckoning

One evening, long after his team had gone home and the city outside had transitioned from the busy hum of day to the quiet twinkle of night, Aryan sat alone in his office. The glow of the desk lamp cast shadows across the room, turning the normally pristine space into a place of reflection and doubt. His desk, once a symbol of control and accomplishment, now seemed to mock him with its meticulous order. How could everything appear so perfect on the outside when his internal world was in turmoil?

The city lights below sparkled like distant stars, but instead of filling Aryan with the usual sense of satisfaction, they only heightened his sense of isolation. The more he tried to force a solution, the more the situation seemed to slip through his fingers. The venture that had once promised so much now felt like a sinking ship, and Aryan, for all his skills and experience, couldn't bail water fast enough.

He stared at the cityscape, feeling the vastness of the world outside his window—a world that kept spinning, indifferent to his personal struggle. The calm, orderly exterior he had maintained for so long was beginning to crack, and behind it, he felt a deep, gnawing sense of inadequacy. For the first time in a long time, Aryan faced the possibility that he might not be able to fix this, that his carefully constructed world of success and achievement might crumble around him.

Turning Point - The Art of Imperfection

Yet, in the midst of this growing despair, something inside Aryan refused to give in. He had faced challenges before, though none quite like this. As he sat there, bathed in the soft glow of the city's lights - Aryan found his mind drifting to a story that had once lingered at the edges of his consciousness. It was the tale of a renowned potter named Anaya, a master artist whose name was synonymous with beauty and craftsmanship. Anaya's creations were celebrated far and wide, not just for their aesthetic appeal, but for something far more profound—her unique relationship with imperfection.

Unlike other artisans, Anaya did not strive for flawlessness in her pottery. In fact, some of her most prized works bore cracks, uneven surfaces, and visible blemishes. But rather than hiding or discarding these pieces, Anaya embraced them. With a delicate touch, she adorned the cracks with intricate inlays of gold and silver, weaving patterns that turned the flaws into features of extraordinary beauty. Her philosophy was simple: perfection wasn't the absence of flaws; it was the ability to transform those flaws into something valuable, something meaningful.

The Lesson in the Clay

Aryan had heard this story before, but its depth had never truly struck him until now, in this moment of solitude and reflection. As he sat amidst the wreckage of his own professional struggle, the parallels between Anaya's approach and his current crisis became glaringly clear.

He had always been the one to seek perfection—the flawless presentation, the ideal outcome, the unblemished path to success. Yet here he was, surrounded by the cracks in his latest project, trying desperately to fix each one, to restore the seamless surface that had once represented his achievements.

But now, something in Aryan shifted. He began to realize that his obsession with achieving perfection had blinded him to a deeper truth. It wasn't about fixing every mistake or eliminating every flaw. It was about learning to embrace those imperfections, to see the value in the cracks, and to adapt with grace.

Just as Anaya had transformed the cracks in her pottery into something beautiful, Aryan began to see that his failures and missteps were not the end of the road, but rather opportunities to grow, to innovate, and to transform. Each missed deadline, each challenge, each moment of frustration was a crack in the surface of his life. But it was within these cracks that the potential for true transformation lay.

Turning Flaws into Features

Aryan's revelation didn't come with a dramatic epiphany or a rush of adrenaline. Instead, it was a quiet, almost imperceptible shift in perspective. The more he reflected on Anaya's approach to her pottery, the more he began to internalize its wisdom. Perfection wasn't about maintaining a flawless facade. It was about finding strength in vulnerability, creativity in limitation, and beauty in imperfection.

With this newfound understanding, Aryan felt a weight lift from his shoulders. The cracks in his project, once symbols of failure, now seemed like places where he could infuse his own artistry—his own inlays of creativity and resilience. The challenges he faced weren't obstacles to be eradicated; they were invitations to innovate, to bring new meaning to the work he had once viewed as broken.

He let the anxiety wash over him, but for the first time, he didn't try to push it away. He acknowledged it, embraced it even, and in doing so, felt a slight loosening of the vise around his chest.

New Perspective Emerges

As the minutes passed, Aryan found clarity in the silence. The project had gone awry, yes, but it was not the end. It was a setback, a detour, a learning experience. The external markers of success—the sleek office, the high-profile clients, the praise—had clouded his vision, distracting him from the deeper truth he had once known success isn't about controlling every outcome. It's about how you navigate the journey, how you rise from the ashes of failure, and, most importantly, how you remain true to yourself in the process.

That night, Aryan left his office not with the answers to fix his project, but with something far more valuable: a renewed sense of purpose. He realized that while the situation felt beyond his control, his reaction to it wasn't. He had the power to change his approach, to lead with presence, to embrace the challenge with grace rather than force.

The next day, as the early morning sun cast its familiar glow across his office once again, Aryan returned not with a plan to salvage the project, but with a mindset to evolve. He was ready to face the storm, not as an adversary to be conquered but as a force to be understood and navigated.

And that made all the difference.

Principle of Acceptance

Aryan approached his work with a newfound perspective. He understood that the challenges he faced were not failures but part of the natural ebb and flow of any significant endeavor. He began to shift his focus from trying to achieve an unattainable ideal to addressing what could be improved and accepting what was beyond his control. This mindset change allowed him to engage with his team and clients in a more open and honest manner.

Aryan decided to have a candid conversation with the client about the project's setbacks. He admitted the difficulties, expressed his commitment to resolving the issues, and outlined a revised plan to move forward. To his surprise, this transparency and humility fostered a sense of trust and collaboration. The client, while disappointed, appreciated Aryan's honesty and the proactive approach to addressing the problems. The project, though far from perfect, began to regain some of its lost momentum.

The Beauty in Imperfection

As Aryan began to embrace the principle of acceptance in his professional life, he found it slowly seeping into his personal world as well. For years, his relentless pursuit of perfection had taken a toll not only on himself but on his relationships. His obsession with success had cost him countless dinners with his family, moments that could have been filled with laughter and warmth, but instead were sacrificed for late-night work and looming deadlines.

It was a realization that hit him hard. The very people he cherished most had become collateral damage in his unyielding quest for achievement. And so, Aryan made a quiet vow to himself—to shift the focus from perfection to presence. He wanted to reconnect with those who mattered, to repair the cracks that had formed in his relationships, and to start living the values he had recently discovered in his journey of mindfulness.

A Family Gathering, Flaws and All

One weekend, Aryan planned a family gathering at his home. For once, his laptop remained closed, and his phone was left on silent. The usual hum of work emails and project deadlines faded into the background as he set his sights on something far more important—his family.

The event, like any family gathering, was far from perfect. The roast chicken was slightly overcooked, his siblings bickered over an old grudge, and there were awkward lulls in conversation as everyone adjusted to the rare sight of Aryan being fully present. Yet, amidst the chaos, Aryan felt something stir inside him—a quiet joy he hadn't experienced in a long time.

It wasn't the polished, picture-perfect evening he had envisioned, but it was real. The laughter, the teasing, the occasional silence—all of it was part of the beautiful messiness that defined family life. For the first time, Aryan wasn't trying to control or perfect the situation; he was simply there, taking it all in, flaws and all.

Chaaya's Drawing: A Lesson in Love

One moment from that evening etched itself deeply into Aryan's heart. His young niece, Chaaya, had been buzzing with excitement, tugging at his sleeve every chance she got. Toward the end of the night, she shyly approached him, holding out a piece of paper with pride shining in her eyes.

It was a drawing – a colorful, albeit uneven, depiction of their family. The lines wobbled, the proportions were off, and the colors spilled outside the borders. Yet, Chaaya's joy was undeniable. She beamed as she handed him her masterpiece, eagerly awaiting his reaction.

Aryan looked at the drawing, his heart swelling with emotion. It wasn't perfect, not in the conventional sense.

But in that moment, Aryan realized something profound. The drawing was perfect in its intent, in the love with which Chaaya had poured herself into creating it. It wasn't about the technical flaws; it was about the sincerity behind the gesture.

He knelt down to Chaaya's level, gently pulling her into a hug. "It's beautiful," he whispered, his voice thick with emotion. And it was. Not because of its artistic merit, but because it represented something far more valuable—the connection, the love, the unfiltered joy of simply being together.

The Power of Acceptance

As Aryan reflected on the evening, he understood that the imperfections—the overcooked chicken, the sibling squabble, the uneven drawing—were not things to be fixed or avoided. They were the very essence of life, of family, of connection. In his years of chasing perfection, he had missed the beauty in these small, imperfect moments.

What mattered wasn't perfection but acceptance. The ability to be fully there, to appreciate the flaws as part of the experience, and to cherish the imperfect moments as opportunities to connect on a deeper, more authentic level.

From that weekend on, Aryan made it a point to apply the lesson of acceptance to all aspects of his life. He stopped striving for flawless interactions and perfect outcomes. Instead, he focused on being present, on embracing and accepting the messiness of life with open arms, and on finding joy in the imperfections that made his relationships, and indeed life itself, so wonderfully real.

And as he did so, Aryan found a sense of fulfillment that he had long been missing. No longer bound by the rigid expectations of perfection, he began to experience the simple, unfiltered joy of just *being*—with his work, with his family, and with himself.

This shift in perspective helped Aryan embrace imperfections in all areas of his life. He began to see mistakes not as failures but as opportunities for growth and learning. His acceptance of the natural ebb and flow of life brought him a profound sense of relief and inner peace. He no longer saw imperfections as threats to his success but as integral elements of his journey.

The Path Forward

As Aryan continued to integrate acceptance into his daily life, he found that it enhanced his overall well-being. He became more resilient in the face of challenges, more compassionate toward himself and others, and more appreciative of the beauty in life's imperfections. The power of acceptance became a cornerstone of his personal and spiritual growth, guiding him toward a deeper sense of fulfillment.

Just as Anaya's pottery was celebrated not for its flawlessness, but for its resilience and transformation, Aryan realized that his journey, too, would be defined not by the absence of struggle, but by how he responded to it. And in that response, he knew, lay the true artistry of life.

Aryan's journey of embracing imperfection and uncertainty marked a significant evolution in his quest for balance and happiness. His newfound ability to accept mistakes and challenges without losing his inner peace prepared him for the next phase of his journey: mastering the art of letting go while still pursuing his goals with purpose and clarity.

Chapter 16

Mastering the Art of Letting Go (Without Giving Up)

"Letting go isn't about giving up; it's about releasing the grip of ego and embracing the flow of life."

Aryan Kapoor had already walked a path few dared to tread, navigating the delicate balance between material wealth and inner peace. He had once been the epitome of corporate success—a man defined by his possessions, his towering ambition, and his relentless pursuit of achievement. But in the quiet spaces between meetings and deadlines, Aryan had discovered something unexpected: the power of mindfulness.

It had transformed his life. He learned to be fully present, to savor the richness of each moment, and to reframe both success and failure as part of a larger, more meaningful journey. What was once a life defined by titles and tangible rewards had evolved into something deeper, more reflective. Aryan found centeredness even amid the chaos of modern life, weaving mindfulness into his every action.

But just when he thought he had mastered the art of balance, life presented him with an even greater challenge. A challenge that, if conquered, would take him beyond the realms of professional success or personal enlightenment. It was the challenge of *letting go*—not of his ambition or drive, but of the attachment to outcomes that once fueled them.

The Crossroads of Ambition and Surrender

Letting go didn't mean giving up, Aryan knew that. It wasn't about abandoning his ambitions or losing the hunger that had driven him to great heights. But it was about freeing himself from the invisible chains of expectation—the belief that his worth was measured solely by the tangible results of his efforts.

At this stage in his journey, Aryan's goals had not diminished. He still envisioned success, still aspired to greater heights. But now, those aspirations came with a sense of detachment. It wasn't indifference; rather, it was a quiet, profound understanding that life's greatest moments often arose when one surrendered the need for control. The outcomes, he realized, would be what they were meant to be.

This realization came at a critical juncture in his life—a moment when he was on the brink of his biggest career decision yet. A new business opportunity had presented itself, one that promised enormous rewards but required enormous risk. In the past, Aryan would have charged ahead, driven by the thrill of the challenge, his mind racing with all the ways he could turn the opportunity into another crowning achievement.

But this time, something was different. Aryan didn't feel the familiar pressure to conquer. Instead, he found himself standing at a crossroads, pausing to reflect on what this opportunity truly meant.

The Weight of Expectation

The old Aryan would have been consumed by the weight of expectation—both from others and from himself. Every decision had once been a test of his worth, a measure of his success. But standing in the stillness of his newfound perspective, Aryan saw things differently.

He knew that whether this opportunity led to victory or failure was no longer the defining factor of his journey. What mattered was the experience itself—the lessons it would teach him, the people it would bring into his life, and the growth it would inspire.

So, he approached this decision with a quiet confidence, unburdened by the need for a specific outcome. He moved forward, not with the rigid determination to succeed, but with a fluid openness to whatever the journey might unfold.

The Paradox of Attachment

The marble floors of Aryan's office gleamed under the polished light, reflecting the many awards and accolades that lined the walls. Each framed achievement was a testament to his hard work and ambition, but Aryan had begun to sense a growing disconnection between his sense of self and these symbols of success. He found himself questioning: Was his identity becoming intertwined with his external achievements? The question stirred a feeling of unease in him, compelling him to delve deeper into his relationship with success and failure.

Reflecting on previous chapters of his journey, Aryan recognized that his quest for inner peace had led him to explore the boundaries between material wealth and spiritual fulfillment. He had embraced mindfulness in his everyday tasks and learned to view his possessions not as measures of his worth but as tools in his journey. Yet, the challenge now was to understand how to achieve balance between his drive for success and the inner tranquility he sought.

A New Perspective on Failure

The air in the boardroom was thick with tension. Aryan Kapoor sat at the head of the long, polished table, his eyes scanning the faces of his team members. Just days ago, they had been riding high on the anticipation of a major product launch—a launch that Aryan had spearheaded with the kind of meticulous detail and passion that had become his hallmark. The stakes were sky-high, the pressure immense. And yet, despite their best efforts, the launch had fallen short of expectations.

Aryan felt a familiar wave of emotions rise within him—frustration, disappointment, and that old companion, self-doubt. But something was different this time. The failure stung, yes, but instead of letting it pull him into a spiral of blame or self-criticism, Aryan felt a quiet determination growing. He was no stranger to setbacks, but in this moment, he realized that he had a choice. He could either let this failure define him, as so many failures had in the past, or he could use it to redefine his approach to success.

As the team gathered for the post-launch debrief, the tension in the room was palpable. In the past, a setback of this magnitude might have led to harsh critiques, finger-pointing, or a sense of collective defeat. But Aryan felt a profound shift within himself. This was not the time to assign blame; this was a moment for transformation.

With a calm that surprised even him, Aryan broke the silence. "We didn't hit the mark," he began, his voice steady but reflective. "And that's okay. What matters now is what we take from this experience."

The team was taken aback. They had expected disappointment, perhaps even reprimands. Instead, Aryan's words opened a new space—one of reflection and learning, rather than judgment.

The Turning Point

Instead of a traditional debrief filled with analysis and critique, Aryan led the team in a different direction. "Let's talk about what we learned," he said, leaning forward. "What didn't work? What could we have done differently? And most importantly, how can we use this setback to fuel our next success?"

What followed was not the dissection of a failure, but a deeply collaborative conversation. Aryan's openness to discussing the shortcomings without harsh judgment created a ripple effect. His vulnerability in acknowledging the disappointment, while also shifting focus to growth and improvement, ignited a spark in his team. People who had once been afraid to speak up for fear of criticism now felt encouraged to share their ideas. They didn't hold back, and Aryan saw the magic of curiosity overtake the room. Ideas began to flow freely, new strategies emerged, and the team—once weighed down by the pressure of perfection—

found themselves liberated by the freedom to experiment, to try, to fail, and to try again.

As the team engaged in this dialogue, Aryan couldn't help but marvel at the transformation taking place—not just within his team, but within himself. This was no longer about salvaging a failed project. It was about evolving beyond failure, using it as a catalyst for deeper insights, and cultivating a mindset of resilience. The setback became a shared lesson in resilience, a reminder that failure was not the end of the road, but a stepping stone on a much longer, richer journey.

For Aryan, the real turning point was internal. This was the moment he realized that success was not about avoiding failure at all costs—it was about facing it head-on, learning from it, and allowing it to propel him toward greater heights. He had always been driven by ambition, but now, his drive was tempered by a newfound wisdom: the understanding that growth often comes not in the moments of triumph, but in the moments when things don't go as planned.

Aryan realized that the failure itself was not the enemy. His past self might have seen it as a roadblock, a blemish on his record, but now he saw it as an opportunity. By embracing failure with curiosity instead of judgment, he found the potential for innovation and creativity in places he never would have looked before.

Ripple Effect

Aryan's shift in perspective didn't go unnoticed. His team, once fearful of mistakes, began to adopt a similar mindset.

They approached future projects with a renewed sense of energy, creativity, and confidence. The pressure to be perfect was replaced by the thrill of exploration. Failures became opportunities for learning, and each setback was a chance to refine their approach.

As the weeks passed, the team's renewed focus led to breakthroughs that had previously seemed out of reach. They tackled their next project with an unshakable confidence, not because they were certain of success, but because they knew that even in failure, they would find value.

The Freedom of Releasing the Ego

Aryan Kapoor's journey toward understanding the role of ego unfolded in a way he had never anticipated—a journey that would change not only how he perceived his success but also how he related to the world around him. As he slipped behind the wheel of his cherished Ferrari, once a mere dream, it had become a symbol of his status, a shiny emblem of achievement and prestige that he had worked so hard to attain. But on this day, something felt different.

As he navigated the bustling streets of the city, the hum of the engine echoed his excitement, but he couldn't shake the feeling that the car had begun to represent more than just a luxury item. It had morphed into a piece of his identity, a marker of who he was in the eyes of others. The realization struck him like a bolt of lightning: the Ferrari, while exquisite, was merely a vehicle—both literally and metaphorically. It was not the essence of Aryan Kapoor; it was simply a part of his life, a tool for navigating the world.

As he cruised along, the rhythm of the city wrapped around him like a warm embrace. The sleek, red exterior turned heads, but instead of reveling in the attention, Aryan found himself contemplating deeper questions. Then, like a sudden pause in the symphony of life, he found himself caught in a traffic jam. What could have been a moment of frustration transformed into an opportunity for introspection. He leaned back in his seat and took a deep breath, allowing the world outside to unfold before him.

In that seemingly mundane moment, Aryan observed the vibrant tapestry of life surrounding him. Families laughed together on the sidewalks, street vendors called out to potential customers, and children chased each other with gleeful abandon. The sounds of the city—the honking horns, the chatter of conversations, the sizzle of food being cooked nearby—created a vivid symphony that painted a picture of human connection and joy.

He began to understand that his life was intertwined with these experiences. He was not merely a businessman in a high-end car; he was part of a greater community, a web of interactions and relationships that defined the richness of his existence. The Ferrari, while a beautiful piece of machinery, was not a measure of his worth but a tool that enabled him to experience life's richness.

With this newfound perspective, Aryan felt a sense of liberation wash over him. He realized that by releasing his attachment to the ego—the need to be seen as successful and superior—he was free to engage more genuinely with the world. He could appreciate the simple joys that life offered without being tethered to the expectations tied to his possessions.

As the traffic began to clear, Aryan made a conscious choice to immerse himself in the moment. He rolled down the window, letting the breeze tousle his hair and fill the car with the intoxicating scent of fresh street food. He waved at a little boy selling colorful balloons, who responded with a wide grin, and for a fleeting moment, Aryan felt a kinship with the child. They both understood joy, albeit from different worlds.

The Shift in Identity

This shift in identity was profound. Aryan no longer felt the need to showcase his success through material possessions. The Ferrari was no longer a symbol of status; it became a means to explore life—an avenue to seek adventure and connect with others. He began to see it as a vessel that could transport him to new experiences rather than an extension of his self-worth.

That evening, as he parked the Ferrari in his driveway, he felt an overwhelming sense of gratitude. He didn't need to impress anyone; he only needed to be true to himself. This realization set the stage for a deeper transformation – a journey of embracing authenticity over appearances, substance over status.

The Irony of Success

Aryan's decision to let go wasn't easy. It went against everything he had once believed in – his need for control, his obsession with results. But in the process, he found something far more valuable: freedom.

Freedom from the anxiety of uncertainty. Freedom from the burden of needing everything to turn out perfectly. Freedom from the invisible handcuffs of expectation that had once dictated his every move.

And as he let go, something incredible happened.

Aryan observed a curious irony - the more he released his grip on the outcome, the more opportunities seemed to flow to him effortlessly.

The success he had once chased so fiercely now came to him naturally, unforced. With each step forward, the universe seemed to reward his openness, aligning him with the right people, ideas, and moments—those that were meant for him.

But perhaps the most profound realization of all was that letting go didn't mean letting go of *himself*. Aryan was still driven, still passionate, still ambitious. But his ambitions no longer controlled him. He was no longer defined by what he achieved or didn't achieve. Instead, he was defined by the authenticity of his efforts and the joy he found in the journey itself.

Chapter 17

Choosing Compassion

"Compassion becomes central to interactions, transforming relationships by leading with kindness and understanding."

The crisp autumn air was tinged with the scent of fallen leaves and the promise of change as Aryan Kapoor strolled through the park near his office. This sanctuary, with its rustling trees and tranquil pathways, had become his refuge—a place to escape the relentless pace of daily life and reflect on the profound shifts within him. As he transitioned from grappling with material success to embracing simplicity, mindfulness, and acceptance, Aryan found clarity in the lessons nature had to offer.

A Moment of Realization

Throughout his career, Aryan had been a man of action, driven by ambition and an unyielding pursuit of excellence. Success had often come at the cost of meaningful connections, and as he stood among the vibrant colors of autumn, he felt a growing disconnection between himself and the people around him. The laughter of children playing in the distance and the sight of couples walking hand in hand reminded him that true fulfillment lay not in solitary achievements but in nurturing the bonds that made life rich.

This epiphany stirred a desire within Aryan to explore compassion as a guiding principle in his life. He recognized that by fostering compassion, he could cultivate a sense of belonging not just for himself but for those around him.

A New Mindset

The morning after his reflective walk in the park, Aryan arrived at his sleek, modern office building, feeling the weight of this newfound awareness. The contrast between the bustling cityscape and the serene park was stark, yet he carried with him a commitment to infuse his work environment with warmth and empathy. Today would be different.

As he walked through the sleek hallways filled with the hum of productivity, Aryan noticed his team immersed in their tasks, their faces a mix of concentration and fatigue. The realization struck him: behind every spreadsheet and project update were individuals with their own stories, struggles, and aspirations. He felt a renewed sense of responsibility—not just as a leader but as a fellow human being.

A Spontaneous Team Meeting

Determined to change the dynamic within his team, Aryan called a spontaneous meeting—an unexpected departure from his usual structured approach. As the team gathered, curiosity and apprehension flickered across their faces. They were used to meetings that dissected targets and strategized for results, but today, Aryan wanted to do something different.

He began the meeting not with an agenda but with gratitude. "I want to take a moment to express my appreciation for all of you," he said, his voice steady and sincere. "I see the hard work, the late nights, and the sacrifices you've made. You're not just a team; you're a vital part of this organization, and your efforts matter."

The impact of Aryan's words was immediate. Priya, a senior team member known for her diligence, had recently been managing a demanding project while coping with a personal crisis. Aryan's recognition of her struggles touched her deeply, a stark contrast to the isolation she had felt behind the professional facade. For the first time, Priya felt seen and valued, her burden lightened by the acknowledgment of her humanity.

A Transformative Office Atmosphere

The shift was palpable. Colleagues who had once worked in silos began openly supporting one another. The office atmosphere transformed from one of competitive pressure to vibrant collaboration. Aryan's act of compassion had set a new tone, fostering a sense of unity and shared purpose that resonated in the quality of their work and the spirit of the office.

The following days were filled with laughter and camaraderie as the team began to bond over shared experiences and collective challenges. The transformation in the workplace was not just about productivity; it was about fostering a culture where empathy thrived, and every individual felt they had a stake in the team's success.

A Shift at Home

Aryan didn't stop at work; he applied the same principles at home. He made a conscious effort to engage with his family more meaningfully, prioritizing connection over distractions. One evening, as he sat at the dinner table with his wife, Meera, and their children, he observed their interactions with fresh eyes.

His son, Aarav, was animatedly discussing a school project. In the past, Aryan might have offered a quick solution or a fleeting acknowledgment before retreating into his own thoughts. But now, he listened intently, asking questions and offering encouragement. "That sounds amazing! What part are you most excited about?" he inquired, his eyes lighting up with genuine interest.

Aarav's eyes sparkled with gratitude as he felt truly heard and valued. Meera noticed the change in Aryan's demeanor; his attentiveness ignited deeper conversations and strengthened their family bond. The laughter and warmth around the dinner table grew, enriching their home life and fostering an atmosphere of love and support.

The Impact of Compassion

One memorable instance of Aryan's commitment to compassion occurred during a weekend community event. He volunteered at a local food bank, where he met Neha, a woman who had recently lost her job and was struggling to support her family. Aryan listened to Neha's story with empathy, offering not just material support but also connecting her with resources that could help her rebuild her life.

Neha's tearful gratitude and the hope in her eyes left a profound impact on Aryan. He realized that the act of compassion was not merely about giving; it was about forming connections that uplifted others. In that moment, Aryan understood that compassion was not a passive sentiment but an active practice requiring intentionality and effort.

Broader Effect

The broader effect of Aryan's newfound compassion extended beyond his immediate circle. He engaged more actively in community initiatives, finding fulfillment in contributing to causes that resonated with him. Whether it was organizing charity events or participating in local clean-up drives, his involvement deepened his connection to the broader world and reinforced the idea that compassion was a bridge between personal contentment and collective well-being.

As he volunteered, Aryan encountered others who were facing challenges and adversities. Each interaction enriched his perspective, reinforcing his commitment to making a difference in the lives of those around him. He began to understand that his role as a leader extended beyond the confines of his office; it was about nurturing a spirit of compassion and kindness within his community.

The Shift

Reflecting on his journey, Aryan recognized that choosing compassion was not merely a new habit but a fundamental shift in perspective. It was a natural extension of his previous realizations about mindfulness, acceptance, and gratitude. Compassion had become a cornerstone of his approach to life, enhancing his relationships and enriching his experiences.

This journey of embracing compassion marked a pivotal transformation for Aryan. It was a seamless progression from his earlier experiences, illuminating a path to achieving a more balanced and fulfilling life. No longer did he chase success in isolation; instead, he found fulfillment in connections, shared experiences, and the simple joys of being present in the lives of others.

The Legacy of Compassion

In the heart of the bustling city, where ambition and competition often overshadow human connection, Aryan Kapoor became a living testament to the power of compassion, a beacon of positivity within his workplace and community, inspiring others to embrace empathy and kindness.

As Aryan continued to cultivate compassion in his life, he discovered that it was a journey without an end—a continuous cycle of learning, growing, and compassionately connecting.

As autumn leaves danced in the wind, Aryan embraced each moment, knowing that in every act of compassion, he was not just transforming himself in his continued journey but also the world around him.

Chapter 18

The Intersection of Mind and Body

"Aligning physical well-being with spiritual goals through practices like yoga enhances the connection between body and spirit."

As Aryan Kapoor ventured deeper into his journey of self-discovery, he realized that the clarity and peace he had achieved through practices of compassion, gratitude, and acceptance were not enough. True harmony required aligning his mind, spirit, and body as he recalled reading somewhere – *"To keep the body in good health is a duty, otherwise we shall not be able to keep our mind strong and clear."* – Buddha

For years, his body had been a secondary priority, sacrificed to the relentless demands of his career. Yet, the pursuit of physical well-being felt inseparable from his spiritual evolution.

Aryan understood that neglecting his body while striving for mental and spiritual clarity was counterproductive. He needed to realign his physical self to fully integrate the insights he had gained.

Yoga: A New Path Toward Alignment

On a crisp autumn morning, Aryan set out to begin his journey toward physical wellness.

He visited a yoga studio that a friend had recommended. Situated in a serene corner of the city, the studio was a tranquil oasis amidst the bustling urban environment.

The moment Aryan entered, he felt an immediate sense of calm, the gentle sound of wind chimes and the soothing aroma of essential oils signaling that he was stepping into a space of healing.

Nora, his yoga instructor, greeted him with warmth. Her serene presence was a refreshing contrast to the high-pressure environments Aryan was used to. Her first words spoke volumes about the journey Aryan was about to embark upon:

"Yoga isn't just about physical poses. It's about aligning the body and mind. When you connect with your breath, you connect with your inner self."

The Struggles of Early Practice

Initially, Aryan found yoga more challenging than expected. His muscles protested, and his mind wandered, filled with the usual stresses of work and unresolved anxieties.

The physical demands were difficult, and the mental discipline required was unfamiliar. Yet, Aryan persisted. He was committed to exploring the deeper connection between his mind and body, even as his muscles ached and his thoughts raced.

Slowly but surely, the practice began to take root. Aryan's body started to soften, and his mind became more present during each session. As he focused on his breath and the subtle movements of his body, he began to experience moments of stillness—both physical and mental.

"The body is your temple. Keep it pure and clean for the soul to reside in." – B.K.S. Iyengar

The Epiphany: Discovering Inner Balance

One evening, during a particularly intense yoga session, Aryan found himself in *Warrior II* (Virabhadrasana II), a pose that demanded unwavering focus, balance, and inner strength. His legs were trembling under the strain of holding the position, his arms extended with precision, and his breath steady but labored. Each inhale and exhale grounded him further into the present moment, pushing away the incessant chatter of his mind. It was as if time had slowed, and in that brief pause, Aryan became acutely aware of his body—every muscle, every sinew, the weight of his feet pressing into the mat, and the controlled tension in his arms as they reached outward.

The physical challenge of holding the pose was undeniable, but something deeper began to unfold. As his body resisted the strain, his mind gradually settled, no longer distracted by the day's worries or the endless demands of his life. In this rare stillness, Aryan experienced a profound shift—a deep connection between his physical strength and his mental clarity. For the first time, he felt the alignment of body, mind, and spirit, all working together in harmony.

In that moment of struggle and focus, it struck Aryan that this was more than just a physical posture. *Warrior II* was not simply about maintaining balance or holding the pose longer than the person next to him. It was symbolic of something greater. His trembling legs symbolized the battles he had fought in his life—through career, ambition, and personal challenges. His arms, stretched wide like wings, reminded him of his potential to reach for something beyond the physical realm. And his steady breath mirrored the growing peace within, a testament to his internal transformation.

It was in *Warrior II* that Aryan realized his body was not just a vehicle to carry him through life's challenges or a tool for achievement. His physical being was an essential part of his spiritual journey, not separate from it. Every muscle, every movement, and every breath had a purpose beyond the physical—it was all part of a greater alignment.

He recalled the ancient yogic wisdom that spoke of the body as the temple of the soul, and in that moment, Aryan truly understood its meaning. Yoga was more than just an exercise or a means to stay fit; it was a gateway to aligning his physical well-being with his spiritual goals. The connection between his body and spirit, which had long been ignored in his pursuit of success, was now undeniable. He realized that the strength of his body could either hinder or enhance his journey toward spiritual fulfillment.

As he stood in that pose, Aryan felt a profound sense of peace. His body, mind, and spirit had converged in perfect alignment. He understood that the discipline required to maintain physical strength and balance mirrored the discipline needed for mental clarity and spiritual growth. Yoga had become the bridge between his inner world and the physical reality he inhabited.

Incorporating Yoga Poses into Daily Life

With renewed focus, as Aryan Kapoor journeyed through his practice of yoga, he found not only physical challenges but also profound emotional and mental struggles that mirrored the inner turbulence of his life.

Each pose became an encounter with his inner world, forcing him to face doubts, insecurities, and unresolved emotions. However, through perseverance and self-awareness, Aryan eventually experienced a deeper awakening – an alignment between his body and spiritual mind. This harmony gradually unfolded as he embraced both the physical challenges of yoga and the emotional confrontations they brought.

Tadasana (Mountain Pose): Struggling with Stillness and Stability

Aryan's initial attempts at *Tadasana* (Mountain Pose) were marked by a surprising challenge. Though the pose appeared simple – standing tall with feet grounded – he felt restless and distracted. His mind raced with thoughts about his professional obligations, future plans, and unresolved conflicts. This inability to remain still frustrated him, triggering a sense of inadequacy.

For Aryan, *Tadasana* became symbolic of his internal battle: a deep-rooted fear of standing still in life, of not making progress. He had always been driven by success, ambition, and constant motion, but here, the challenge was to do nothing – to simply be. As he persisted with this pose, the frustration gradually gave way to acceptance.

Over time, Aryan experienced a shift in his perception. He realized that standing tall in *Tadasana* wasn't about physical posture but about emotional stability. The grounding sensation beneath his feet reminded him that, like a mountain, he could remain firm and unshaken even amidst the chaos of life. It was a subtle yet profound awakening: stillness could be a source of strength, not stagnation.

Balasana (Child's Pose): Confronting Vulnerability

When Aryan first encountered *Balasana* (Child's Pose), he approached it as a retreat, a resting pose during intense yoga sessions. However, as he folded forward with his arms stretched out, he began to experience feelings of vulnerability and a surprising emotional release. He had spent much of his life projecting strength and control, always striving to appear invincible to others. But in *Balasana*, he found himself face to face with his own vulnerability.

At first, this realization frightened him. Lying there, forehead pressed to the mat, he felt small, exposed, and defenseless. Memories of times when he had been hurt or disappointed surfaced. The quiet of the pose amplified the inner noise of unresolved fears and insecurities. Aryan wanted to escape, to move out of the pose and into something more challenging that would distract him.

But something kept him in *Balasana*. He understood that surrendering was not a sign of weakness. Slowly, he allowed himself to release the need for control. He stopped resisting his emotions and began to accept them, realizing that vulnerability was a necessary part of growth. Through this acceptance, Aryan experienced a deep sense of peace. The pose became his space for reflection, teaching him that true strength comes not from denying one's fragility but from embracing it fully.

Vrksasana (Tree Pose): Struggling for Balance

When Aryan first attempted *Vrksasana* (Tree Pose), he wobbled, lost balance, and had to place his foot back on the ground. This simple act of standing on one leg with the other foot pressed against his thigh seemed deceptively difficult. As he swayed and stumbled, frustration bubbled up within him. He had always prided himself on his ability to stay in control, yet here he was, unable to maintain balance in a pose that appeared so basic.

But *Vrksasana* mirrored Aryan's deeper struggle – the challenge of finding balance in his life. Professionally, he had been successful, but emotionally and spiritually, he often felt out of sync. The balancing act on the mat reminded him of the delicate equilibrium he sought between his material ambitions and his inner peace.

As Aryan practiced *Tree Pose* day after day, he began to understand that balance was not about being perfect or never faltering. Instead, it was about making constant, subtle adjustments. Whenever he wavered in the pose, he realigned his focus, engaged his core, and grounded himself more deeply. In doing so, he realized that life, like *Vrksasana*, required continuous recalibration.

Over time, Aryan experienced a shift in mindset. The act of wobbling was no longer a source of frustration but an opportunity for growth. He became more forgiving of himself when he lost balance, understanding that stability was a journey, not a destination. This newfound perspective was a significant breakthrough in his self-realization journey – finding peace in the process of balancing rather than seeking perfection.

Shavasana (Corpse Pose): Facing the Fear of Letting Go

Shavasana (Corpse Pose) proved to be Aryan's greatest challenge—not physically, but mentally and emotionally. Lying still at the end of each yoga session, Aryan found it difficult to relax. His mind would race, reviewing the day's events or planning the future. He struggled to let go, to fully surrender into the pose.

At first, *Shavasana* felt uncomfortable. Aryan was so accustomed to being active, to striving and achieving, that the idea of simply lying still felt foreign to him. Yet, as he forced himself to remain in the pose, something within him began to shift. Slowly, the constant chatter of his mind began to quiet down.

In *Shavasana*, Aryan confronted his deepest fear – the fear of letting go. He realized that much of his life had been spent holding on – to expectations, to goals, to control. But lying in stillness, with nothing to do but breathe, he began to understand that true freedom comes from release.

It was in this final pose that Aryan found the deepest sense of alignment between his body, mind, and spirit.

In *Shavasana*, Aryan experienced a profound awakening. Letting go was not about giving up or losing something. It was about creating space for new possibilities to emerge. By releasing his need for control, Aryan found peace, not just in the pose, but in his life as a whole.

Each practice complemented the other, creating a synergy that enhanced his overall well-being.

His physical health improved. His body became stronger and more flexible, and his energy levels increased. But more importantly, Aryan began to experience a profound sense of balance in all areas of his life. The connection between his mind, body, and spirit became more integrated, and his overall lifestyle transformed.

Commitment to Holistic Wellness

Inspired by his own experiences, Aryan committed himself to a holistic approach to wellness. He no longer viewed yoga as merely a physical exercise but as a vital part of his spiritual journey. He recognized that his body and mind were not separate entities but intertwined aspects of his existence that needed to be nurtured equally.

Weeks turned into months, and Aryan witnessed a profound transformation. Not only did his body grow stronger and more flexible, but his mind also became clearer and more focused. His sleep improved, his stress levels decreased, and he found a deep sense of peace that permeated all areas of his life.

The integration of his physical and spiritual practices had brought about a new level of harmony. Aryan realized that by taking care of his body, he was enhancing his spiritual growth. The connection between his physical well-being and his inner peace had become undeniable.

The Intersection of Mind and Body: A Lifelong Journey

As Aryan reflected on his journey, he understood that the intersection of mind and body was not a one-time revelation but a continuous process. Maintaining balance between his physical, mental, and spiritual selves required ongoing attention and care.

Yoga had served as the bridge that connected these aspects of his life, allowing him to experience true harmony. *"When the breath wanders, the mind is unsteady. But when the breath is calmed, the mind too will be still."* – Hatha Yoga Pradipika

Aryan's commitment to physical wellness wasn't just about health; it was about alignment. His physical well-being was now an essential part of his spiritual journey, enriching his life in ways he hadn't anticipated. The integration of mind and body had become a fundamental pillar of his transformation, leading him toward a more balanced, fulfilled existence.

Chapter 19

Living with Intention

"Making mindful choices and focusing on what truly matters helps in saying 'no' to distractions and 'yes' to what fosters inner peace."

The morning sun bathed Aryan Kapoor's garden in a soft, golden light, the warmth melting away the lingering chill from the night. Each blade of dewy grass shimmered like a tiny jewel, reflecting the new day's promise. Aryan sat quietly on a wooden bench, cradling a cup of herbal tea. The steam curled up in lazy spirals, and he inhaled deeply, feeling the calm settle within him. For years, he had been a man driven by the ticking of clocks and the chase for more—more success, more status, more everything. But here, in this moment, it all felt so distant, almost foreign. The stillness that now enveloped him was something he had never allowed himself to experience before.

He gazed out at the meticulously tended flower beds, where every petal seemed to sway in sync with the gentle rustle of the leaves in the breeze. Each sound, each sight grounded him further in the present. The hum of his once-hectic life had faded into an almost forgotten memory, replaced by a profound sense of clarity. For the first time, Aryan was able to truly savor these quiet moments without the incessant need to rush toward something undefined.

His journey to this point had been anything but linear. It was a path marked by mindfulness, compassion, and a reconnection to his physical and spiritual self. Yet today, seated in his serene sanctuary, he understood that it wasn't just about slowing down. *It was about reshaping his life with a sense of purpose, with deliberate intention.* The old Aryan had thrived in chaos, but the new Aryan was finding strength in simplicity.

He sipped his tea, contemplating the monumental shift he had undergone. This wasn't a fleeting change or a temporary pause. It was a complete redefinition of his existence. Living with intention, Aryan realized, wasn't just about stripping away the distractions that had once cluttered his days. It was about a deep, almost spiritual realignment of his values. It meant prioritizing inner peace over outward validation, cherishing the beauty in simplicity rather than striving for complexity.

Aryan's introspection deepened as he took in his surroundings, the simplicity of the garden mirroring the richness of his inner world. Here, amid the flowers and the soft rustling leaves, he had found something far more valuable than any accolade or achievement. He had found himself.

Redefining Priorities

Aryan's journey toward intentional living began with a simple yet profound step: reimagining his daily routines. His schedule, once a chaotic whirlwind of meetings, deadlines, and social commitments, now stood before him as a blank canvas, waiting for careful and deliberate strokes of purpose. No longer content with the mindless busyness that had once filled his days, Aryan began a meticulous reassessment, scrutinizing every activity and asking himself one crucial question—did this align with his true values, or was it just filling time?

The result was a radical realignment. Gone were the obligations that drained his energy and distracted him from his goals. In their place, Aryan crafted a daily plan that prioritized activities nurturing his personal growth. What had once been a checklist of tasks transformed into a pathway toward deeper fulfillment. His mornings, once hurried and chaotic, now began with stillness. These quiet moments became a grounding force, helping him center his thoughts before the world's demands crept in.

As the days passed, Aryan started to carve out time for the things that truly mattered. His well-being became a priority, no longer relegated to the sidelines. Leisurely walks in nature, something he had once considered a luxury, now became essential. The sights, sounds, and sensations of the outdoors helped him reconnect with the world in a more profound way. His creative pursuits, long stifled by the demands of his former life, reemerged, filling him with a sense of purpose and joy.

But perhaps most transformative was how Aryan deepened his relationships. Time spent with loved ones was no longer rushed or obligatory; it was intentional and meaningful. Conversations became richer, and connections, once taken for granted, were now cherished.

Every day became a deliberate act of intention. Aryan's routine no longer felt like a series of tasks to be checked off but a meaningful journey, where each moment was infused with purpose. By stripping away the unnecessary and embracing what truly nourished his soul, Aryan discovered the freedom that came with intentional living. The changes in his schedule reflected a much deeper transformation—his life had shifted from one of constant striving to one of conscious being. And with every choice he made, he grew closer to the person he was truly meant to become.

Transforming Work Dynamics

Aryan's transformation seeped into his approach to work, redefining how he viewed success and leadership. Gone were the days of relentless pursuit for external validation, the constant need to prove his worth through accomplishments and accolades.

Aryan no longer saw work as a means to an end, but as an extension of his values. He began to lead with authenticity and compassion, allowing these qualities to guide his decisions and interactions.

This shift was profound. Aryan had always been a respected leader, but now he was something more—he became a leader who inspired not just results, but a sense of purpose within his team. His focus moved away from rigid metrics and toward fostering a culture where collaboration, empathy, and mindfulness became the cornerstones of success.

His leadership style evolved into something that went beyond managing tasks. He saw the potential in each of his team members and sought to empower them, recognizing that when people felt valued, they naturally performed at their best.

Aryan introduced a new practice that supported this vision - He implemented regular mindfulness breaks, where the team could step back from the demands of work and recalibrate their focus. These pauses, though brief, became essential in keeping everyone grounded and refreshed, preventing burnout while boosting creativity.

Collaboration became the heart of his team's dynamic. Aryan knew that no great innovation or solution came from isolation. He fostered an environment where every voice mattered, where the best ideas were born not from competition, but from collective effort. By encouraging his team to work with intention, he gave them the freedom to explore new ways of thinking, which in turn sparked creativity and ingenuity.

Under Aryan's guidance, the office transformed from a place of sheer productivity to one of holistic well-being. By leading with empathy and supporting his team's mental and emotional health, Aryan created a workplace where people were not only more engaged but also genuinely happy.

The results were undeniable. Projects ran smoothly, ideas flourished, and the team worked with a sense of purpose that transcended deadlines and KPIs. Aryan's shift from a results-driven mindset to one that prioritized living with intention didn't just transform him—it transformed everyone around him. He had built not just a team, but a community where creativity, compassion, and success coexisted harmoniously.

The Art of Saying "No"

One of the most transformative skills Aryan cultivated on his journey was the art of saying "no."

For years, he had been the type to say "yes" to almost everything, driven by an underlying fear—fear of missing out, fear of being seen as unreliable, or fear of disappointing those around him. His calendar was always overflowing, filled with events, projects, and social engagements that left him drained and disconnected from his true purpose. Saying "yes" had become a reflex, one that eroded his sense of self over time.

But as Aryan delved deeper into his practice of intentional living, he began to see "no" not as a rejection, but as an affirmation of his priorities.

He realized that every time he said "yes" to something that didn't align with his values or goals, he was, in essence, saying "no" to something that did. This realization was a turning point. Learning to set boundaries became a liberating practice, one that allowed him to protect his energy and focus on what truly mattered.

At first, saying "no" felt uncomfortable. Aryan had to confront the inner voice that equated declining an invitation or turning down a project with letting someone down. But with each conscious decision to choose himself and his priorities, it became easier. He began by declining events that didn't resonate with his personal growth or align with his vision for the future. Social gatherings that once felt obligatory no longer had a hold over him. If an event didn't bring joy, inspiration, or meaningful connection, Aryan gracefully opted out.

The same went for work projects. In the past, he would take on every assignment, every challenge, believing that busyness was a badge of honor. Now, Aryan understood that true productivity wasn't about doing more but doing what mattered most. He declined tasks that pulled him away from his core focus, using his time more deliberately to dive deeper into projects that ignited his passion and fostered his growth.

What made Aryan's ability to say "no" so impactful was how he approached it—with kindness and clarity.

Each "no" was delivered thoughtfully, without harshness or guilt. He didn't reject opportunities out of avoidance or indifference; instead, he saw every decision as a conscious choice to live more intentionally. When Aryan turned something down, it wasn't because he couldn't handle it or didn't care—it was because he had made a deliberate commitment to honor his values and priorities.

In saying "no" to what no longer served him, Aryan found more space to say "yes" to what truly mattered. His time and energy were no longer scattered across commitments that left him unfulfilled. Instead, he was able to invest deeply in the areas of his life that brought him joy, meaning, and purpose. What once felt like a loss—the missed opportunities, the unmet expectations of others— now felt like freedom.

The art of saying "no" allowed Aryan to reclaim his life, not just as a series of obligations but as a deliberate, intentional journey toward his highest self.

Embracing - to Live With Intention

Aryan's daily life had transformed into a beautiful tapestry of mindful choices, each one woven with deliberate intent.

Gone were the days of rushing through tasks or mindlessly going through the motions. Now, whether he was tackling personal interactions or professional responsibilities, Aryan approached everything with a heightened sense of purpose and awareness. Each moment became an opportunity to be fully present, to engage deeply with life rather than let it pass by in a blur.

Even in moments of challenge, Aryan stayed true to his commitment to intentional living. Life, after all, still presented its fair share of unexpected obstacles and demanding situations. But instead of reacting with frustration or anxiety, Aryan met these moments with a calm, composed mindset. He had learned to practice patience and resilience, viewing each difficulty as an opportunity for growth rather than a source of stress. It wasn't always easy, but by focusing on the bigger picture, Aryan found that even the toughest situations held valuable lessons for him.

By aligning his tasks with his values, Aryan found purpose in his daily responsibilities. But the most profound change was in Aryan's overall sense of well-being. He no longer felt like he was merely surviving from one day to the next. Instead, he was thriving, rooted in a deep sense of peace and clarity. This wasn't a fleeting state of happiness, but an enduring, grounded sense of contentment that came from living with intention. His spiritual practices—once something he did in the quiet hours of morning or evening—had become seamlessly integrated into every facet of his life.

As Aryan continued to embody the principles of intentional living, the effects of his choices began to ripple through every corner of his life. His relationships flourished—both personal and professional—fueled by his genuine presence and empathy.

People around him noticed the shift, drawn to the calmness and clarity he exuded. The clarity and peace he cultivated began to inspire those around him. His leadership at work, his relationships with loved ones, and even the way he moved through the world began to reflect the inner transformation he had undergone.

A Bridge Between Past and Future

This evolution in Aryan's journey wasn't just about personal growth; it served as a bridge between his past and his future. His past experiences—the relentless pursuit of success, the burnout, the constant pressure to meet others' expectations—had all led him to this pivotal point. But rather than reject his past, Aryan embraced it as the foundation that allowed him to make these shifts. It was through the trials and challenges of his earlier life that he had learned the importance of intentional living, and now, with that wisdom in hand, he stood at the edge of a new phase.

With a sense of excitement and anticipation, Aryan looked toward the future, knowing that the practices and mindset he had cultivated would guide him forward. He no longer felt pulled in a hundred different directions, trying to live up to external standards. Instead, he faced the future with clarity, ready to embrace whatever came next, confident that his commitment to living with intention would continue to bring him peace, fulfillment, and growth.

In Aryan's heart, the realization had solidified: this was just the beginning of an even greater journey. A journey where every step, every choice, would be made with purpose and meaning. And as he stood at the threshold of this new chapter, he knew that the best was yet to come.

Chapter 20

Spirituality in the Fast Lane

"Spirituality isn't about retreating from the world; it's about mastering the art of living fully within it."

Aryan Kapoor was no stranger to the exhilarating realm of luxury and ambition, where every moment pulsed with excitement. His Ferrari wasn't just a car; it was an emblem of his relentless pursuit of success, a sleek machine that mirrored his high-octane lifestyle. Yet, as he embarked on a transformative journey toward spiritual awakening, Aryan came to a profound realization: spirituality wasn't about retreating from the fast lane or abandoning the vibrant life he had crafted.

Instead, he discovered that spirituality could thrive alongside his ambitions, providing him with a refreshing perspective on life. It became clear that this inner exploration wasn't a distraction; it was a powerful ally that enriched his experiences. By embracing spirituality, Aryan learned to cultivate a deep sense of inner peace and balance, even as he navigated the exhilarating whirlwind of his high-speed existence.

With newfound excitement, he set out to harmonize his spiritual journey with his ambitious lifestyle, proving that tranquility and ambition could not only coexist but flourish together. Aryan was ready to embrace the thrill of life while nurturing his soul, embarking on a path where both luxury and spirituality intertwined beautifully.

The Road to Mindful Speed

On a brisk autumn morning, with golden leaves dancing in the crisp air, Aryan Kapoor felt a surge of excitement. It was the perfect day to take his beloved Ferrari out for a drive—not just for the thrill of speed, but as a conscious practice of mindfulness. As he slid into the driver's seat, the sleek, red sports car roared to life, its engine purring with raw power.

With each turn of the key, Aryan felt the adrenaline coursing through his veins, but this time, he aimed to transform that energy into something deeper. He wasn't merely chasing the rush; he was ready to immerse himself fully in the experience. The winding roads ahead, adorned with a vibrant tapestry of colorful foliage, beckoned him to explore not just the world around him but the world within.

As he began his journey, Aryan practiced a unique form of dynamic meditation. He synchronized his breath with the rhythm of the engine, inhaling as he accelerated and exhaling during each deceleration. This mindful breathing deepened his connection to the car and the road, allowing him to feel every surge of power and the gentle curves of the asphalt beneath him. The road, stretching out before him, transformed from a mere path into a metaphor for his life—a living entity that responded to his touch and presence. The winding roads, adorned with the fiery hues of autumn, became more than just a path; they symbolized the journey of his life—a living entity that responded to his presence. As he navigated each curve, Aryan allowed himself to let go of the past and the future, embracing the now. The leaves fluttered like confetti in the wind, celebrating his newfound awareness.

With each twist and turn, the sensation of speed evolved. What had once represented ego and ambition now served as a tool for enhancing his mindfulness practice. Aryan began to recognize the profound connection between his physical movements and the serenity blossoming within him. The wind whipped through his hair, a reminder of the freedom he sought, and the sun bathed him in warmth, igniting a sense of connection with the world around him. Each moment felt alive, electric with possibility, as he found harmony in the juxtaposition of exhilaration and tranquility.

Even when faced with unexpected obstacles—an abrupt curve or a sudden change in traffic—Aryan maintained his focus on intentional living. He approached each challenge with a calm and composed mindset, seeing them as opportunities for growth rather than sources of stress. By embracing discomfort and remaining present, he cultivated patience and resilience, reinforcing the idea that inner peace can thrive amid chaos.

This integration of spirituality into a high-speed experience reinforced Aryan's realization that serenity could be discovered even in the whirlwind of modern life. Each mile driven was not just a distance covered but a moment savored, a reminder that mindfulness could coexist beautifully with the exhilaration of living fully.

As Aryan drove on, the autumn sun began to dip lower in the sky, casting a warm, golden glow over the landscape. He felt a sense of gratitude for this journey—both on the road and within himself. The harmony he had discovered in that Ferrari, where spirituality met speed, was a testament to the beauty of living with intention. With each passing moment, he celebrated the art of mindful speed, knowing that true mastery lay in his ability to dance gracefully between ambition and serenity, all while enjoying the ride.

The Gala and the Lesson from the Bhagavad Gita

Aryan's life was a whirlwind of activity, a dazzling tapestry woven with threads of glamour and high-profile engagements. One evening, he found himself attending a charity gala organized by his wife, Meera. The venue was nothing short of spectacular, adorned with glittering chandeliers that cast a warm glow over the room, creating an ambiance of opulence and social grandeur. As Aryan mingled with influential figures, the air buzzed with laughter, music, and the clinking of glasses, forming a vibrant backdrop against which connections were forged and dreams discussed.

Amidst the excitement, Aryan engaged in a conversation with an esteemed guest, a wise elder who had dedicated much of his life to studying ancient texts. Their dialogue meandered through various topics until the guest shared a few shlokas or passages from the Bhagavad Gita that struck a profound chord within Aryan. The passage was from Chapter 2, Verse 47:

"You have a right to perform your prescribed duties, but you are not entitled to the fruits of your actions. Never consider yourself to be the cause of the results of your activities, nor be attached to inaction."

This teaching emphasized the importance of performing one's duties without attachment to the results. Aryan realized that while he could enjoy the luxurious aspects of his life and pursue success, he needed to detach from the obsession with outcomes.

Another shloka that resonated was from Chapter 5, Verse 10:

"He who performs his duty without attachment, surrendering the results unto the Supreme Lord, is unaffected by sinful action, as the lotus leaf is untouched by water."

This insight reinforced Aryan's belief that he could immerse himself in the hustle and bustle of his life while remaining untouched by the stresses and pressures that often accompany ambition. It became clear to him that spirituality isn't about retreating from the world; it's about mastering the art of living fully within it.

As Aryan navigated the lively atmosphere of the gala, he consciously practiced what he had just experienced during his conversation with the guest, integrating it seamlessly into the exhilarating experience of living fully. With every laughter-filled conversation, he took a moment to absorb the joy around him. He reveled in the colors of the room, the laughter of friends, and the warmth of human connection. This heightened awareness allowed him to savor the richness of the moment while remaining grounded in the present. The evening soon became a celebration of connection and contribution rather than a pursuit of personal gain.

As the night progressed, Aryan left the gala feeling uplifted and inspired. The words from the Bhagavad Gita echoed in his mind, guiding him toward a more intentional way of living. He recognized that true fulfillment comes not from accolades or fruits of success but from the act of engaging fully with life, performing his duties with integrity, and embracing the unpredictable nature of existence.

Finding Harmony in the Fast Lane

As Aryan Kapoor navigated the exhilarating landscape of his life, he found himself at a crossroads—one where ambition met spirituality, and the fast lane of his career could coexist with the tranquility he had long sought. His journey was not just about accumulating wealth and accolades; it was about discovering a deeper purpose, an integration of his fast-paced lifestyle without losing sight of the inner peace that had become his guiding star.

Aryan discovered that the exhilaration of living fully did not have to come at the expense of his peace. Instead, they could be intertwined—each success celebrated as a moment of joy, each setback embraced as a lesson in resilience. He recalled Chapter 2, Verse 50, from the Bhagavad Gita.

"A person who is not disturbed by the dualities of happiness and distress, and is unbothered by the results of their work, is certainly eligible for liberation."

This understanding deepened his resolve to cultivate an environment where both ambition and tranquility thrived. As he continued to weave the teachings of the Gita into his life.

Aryan discovered that spirituality wasn't a retreat from the fast lane; it was the very essence that fueled his drive. He began to see every interaction as an opportunity to uplift others, every challenge as a chance to showcase resilience, and every success as a moment to reflect and give thanks.

His weekends became dedicated to nurturing his spiritual practice, whether through quiet reflection, engaging in community service, or exploring nature. These moments of solitude and connection reinforced his understanding that life was a delicate balance—a dance between ambition and mindfulness, between striving for excellence and finding joy in the journey itself.

Aryan Kapoor had not only found harmony in the fast lane; he had become a living testament to the idea that success is not merely about the destination but about how one travels the path. With each mindful choice he made, Aryan felt himself evolving into a new version of himself— one who embraced the complexities of life with an open heart and a curious mind.

This newfound perspective ignited a spark, and the thrill of the journey became as significant as the goals themselves. Aryan was now more than eager to continue his journey, ready to embrace whatever his journey might bring.

Chapter 21

The Power of Presence

"Embracing the present moment fully, joy is found in savoring each experience, whether in daily activities or special moments with loved ones."

The golden hue of dusk enveloped Aryan Kapoor's Ferrari as he parked it beneath the sprawling oak tree in his driveway, its glossy red exterior catching the fading light. The car, once a gleaming testament to his insatiable ambition and relentless pursuit of success, now held a different meaning for him. It was no longer just a symbol of achievement but a reminder of how far he had come in his journey toward balance and self-awareness.

As Aryan sat in the driver's seat, the engine's low hum fading into the stillness of the evening, he found himself reflecting on the transformation that had quietly taken root within him. His hands, once tightly gripping the wheel with urgency, now rested gently, as though they too had learned the art of letting go. He closed his eyes, taking in the moment—not in haste, not as a fleeting pause between destinations, but as a precious fragment of the present, full of life and significance.

The evening breeze rustled the leaves of the oak tree above him, and Aryan breathed deeply, feeling as if the world around him was moving in sync with his own inner rhythms. The once-intimidating silence of slowing down had become a sanctuary, a space where clarity thrived. In that quiet interlude, Aryan realized how much he had evolved. Life had once been about racing forward, always chasing the next milestone, the next goal. Now, he found solace in the act of being still, of simply being present.

As the sun dipped below the horizon, casting long shadows across the driveway, Aryan smiled. The Ferrari, though a marvel of speed and power, had become a vessel for something far greater—a vehicle for mindfulness, for appreciation, for peace. In this tranquil moment, he savored the interplay between ambition and serenity, understanding that they could coexist in harmony. Aryan no longer saw his car as an extension of his ego but as a partner on a much deeper journey—a journey that was no longer about conquering the road ahead but about fully embracing the path he was on.

Power of Presence

The dusk carried with it a sense of completeness, and Aryan allowed himself to soak in the beauty of this transition. It wasn't just the end of a day, but a reminder of the power of presence—a force far more profound than any ambition he had ever chased. In this stillness, he realized that the true measure of success lay not in how fast he could conquer his goals but in how deeply he could engage with each moment along the way. The Ferrari, once a symbol of speed and power, had now become a metaphor for his life's journey—where the true power lay not in acceleration but in presence.

Aryan no longer sought to outpace the world; instead, he embraced the richness that came from being fully present, whether it was in the boardroom, at a charity gala, or in quiet moments like this, parked beneath an oak tree as the day softly ended. His evolving understanding of mindfulness didn't slow him down; it gave him a new kind of power—one that made every moment, every breath, every step, an integral part of his journey. With this newfound awareness, Aryan realized he could move forward not with haste, but with purpose, finding success and serenity woven into the very fabric of his daily life.

Rediscovering Joy in the Ordinary

As Aryan Kapoor's journey deepened, he began to notice something remarkable—the joy he once chased in grand achievements and milestones was quietly present in the most ordinary moments of life.

The power of presence, which had allowed him to find balance in the fast lane, now extended into every facet of his day, transforming even the simplest tasks into moments of fulfillment.

Morning rituals, which once felt like a mere task, became a source of quiet contentment; a reminder that joy doesn't always need to be sought—it often exists in the simplest, most overlooked corners of life.

Even mundane routines, like his evening commute or weekly grocery shopping, took on a new dimension. Instead of viewing them as chores or necessary evils, Aryan engaged with them fully, experiencing them with fresh eyes. Driving through familiar streets, he now noticed the play of sunlight through the trees, the rhythm of pedestrians, the subtle hum of life unfolding around him. The power of presence had awakened his senses to the beauty in the ordinary.

The more Aryan embraced the ordinary, the more extraordinary his life became. Tasks that once felt trivial were now layered with meaning, and he found that, in slowing down and paying attention, there was a richness in every experience. Washing dishes became a chance to clear his mind; walking through a busy market became an opportunity to practice mindfulness amidst chaos. **Each moment offered a chance to rediscover joy, not in the final outcome, but in the act itself.**

In embracing the power of presence, Aryan rediscovered the joy that had always been waiting for him in the simple, everyday moments. He realized that life's true treasures weren't always hidden in grand achievements, but were often scattered throughout the ordinary, waiting to be noticed. In slowing down, he was finally able to appreciate the vibrancy of life in its most subtle forms, and in doing so, he found a new kind of fulfillment—one that didn't rely on future successes, but on the joy of living fully in the present.

This rediscovery of joy in the ordinary allowed Aryan to continue his ambitious journey with a new perspective—one where both his external accomplishments and internal peace coexisted beautifully, each enriching the other. The power of presence had not only brought tranquility to his fast-paced life but had also revealed the magic that resides in the simple, everyday moments that make life truly extraordinary.

A Serendipitous Encounter

One evening, Aryan decided to take his Ferrari for a drive through the countryside. The sun was beginning its descent, casting a warm, golden light over the landscape. As he navigated the winding roads, he let go of all distractions. The soft hum of the engine and the gentle breeze created a symphony of calm. Aryan was fully present, savoring each moment of the journey.

As Aryan Kapoor steered his Ferrari down a winding road, the hum of the engine harmonized with the stillness of the countryside. The sun hung low on the horizon, casting long, golden shadows across the landscape. Just as he thought of heading back, a small village nestled between the hills caught his eye. It seemed almost hidden, like a forgotten painting waiting to be discovered. On impulse, Aryan decided to stop and explore, feeling a quiet pull toward this place that exuded simplicity and charm.

The village was like stepping into another world—one untouched by the rush of modern life. Cobblestone streets crisscrossed between quaint cottages adorned with ivy, and gardens bloomed with vibrant flowers that seemed to spill out from every corner. The pace of life here was noticeably different, slower, more deliberate. As Aryan walked through the village, he couldn't help but feel a sense of calm wash over him, as if the very air invited him to pause and breathe.

Drawn by the smell of freshly baked bread, Aryan wandered into a small, rustic bakery. Inside, the warm, earthy scent of yeast and flour greeted him. Behind the counter, a woman with silver hair tied in a loose bun was kneading dough with steady, practiced hands. Her movements were rhythmic and deliberate, as if each push and fold of the dough was an art form. The woman introduced herself as Clara, and there was a quiet wisdom in her presence, a peace that radiated from her as naturally as the warmth from the oven.

Intrigued by her aura of contentment, Aryan struck up a conversation. He complimented her bread and asked how long she had been in the business. Clara smiled warmly, her eyes twinkling with life, and began to share her story. She spoke of how she had left behind a bustling corporate career years ago to live in this quiet village, dedicating herself to something simpler—baking bread. But it wasn't just about making bread for her; it was a form of meditation.

"Each loaf is a journey," Clara said, her hands still working the dough with gentle precision. "I feel the texture, the weight, the changes with every turn and fold. It's a practice of being fully present, of giving my attention to the moment and nothing else."

Her words resonated deeply with Aryan. He watched her work, noticing the care she poured into each movement, and realized that Clara had found something many people spend their lives searching for—a sense of peace and fulfillment in the ordinary. Clara wasn't chasing external success or validation. She was content because she had found joy in the simplicity of her work, in being present for each moment.

As they continued to talk, Aryan shared some of his own journey, describing the high-speed life he had built and his more recent efforts to slow down, to find meaning beyond material success. Clara listened thoughtfully, then offered him a piece of bread, still warm from the oven. "It's all about the process, not the result," she said softly, echoing one of the teachings Aryan had encountered in his spiritual studies. "When you're truly present, even kneading dough can be a source of joy."

The conversation with Clara struck a chord in Aryan. Here, in this unassuming village bakery, he found the embodiment of everything he had been learning—clarity, peace, and the art of mindful presence. Clara's life, filled with the simple act of baking bread, was a testament to the idea that true contentment didn't require grand achievements or constant motion. It was about being fully engaged in whatever task was at hand, whether that was driving a Ferrari down an open road or kneading dough in a quiet village kitchen.

As Aryan left the bakery, holding the loaf of bread Clara had gifted him, he felt an overwhelming sense of gratitude. This encounter had opened his eyes further to the possibility of finding joy in the small, everyday moments. Clara had shown him that contentment wasn't something to be chased; it was something to be cultivated in the here and now. Aryan realized that while ambition and success were part of who he was, they didn't define him. He could find balance and fulfillment in the ordinary, just as Clara had.

Driving away from the village, Aryan couldn't help but reflect on how much his perspective had shifted.

What had started as a simple detour had turned into a profound reminder that spirituality and ambition weren't mutually exclusive. The power of presence, the ability to fully experience each moment, was the key to rediscovering joy in both the fast and the slow lanes of life. Aryan was beginning to see that his journey wasn't just about achieving success but about living fully—embracing both the extraordinary and the ordinary with equal wonder.

A Reflection on Raj's Wisdom

Aryan's journey into mindfulness often brought his thoughts back to Raj, his old friend. The lessons Raj had shared, once met with skepticism, now resonated deeply within him. Aryan chuckled to himself as he remembered how he used to dismiss Raj's calm demeanor and musings on the power of the present as 'impractical' in the fast-paced world they lived in. To Aryan then, success was measured in results and achievements, not in the stillness of the mind or the appreciation of fleeting moments. But now, he had come to realize just how much wisdom Raj's words truly held.

One particular conversation stood out in Aryan's memory. Raj had spoken softly but with conviction. "The present moment," he had said, "is the only reality we truly have. The past is gone, and the future is uncertain. But this moment, right here and now, is where life happens. Embrace it fully, and you will find peace."

At the time, Aryan had nodded politely, thinking Raj's words were wise but impractical for someone with as many responsibilities and ambitions as he had. "How can one stay present," Aryan had thought, "when there are deadlines to meet, deals to close, and goals to achieve?"

Now, after his experiences on the road of life—both literal and metaphorical—Aryan understood - it wasn't about abandoning ambition or rejecting success, but about finding presence within the pursuit.

A deep sense of gratitude washed over Aryan. He was thankful for Raj's quiet wisdom and for the subtle way those teachings had influenced his path.

Returning Home: Aryan's Reflection on Presence

As Aryan returned home, the soft hum of his Ferrari fading into the evening air, his mind was alive with reflection. The serene encounter with Clara, the lessons from Raj, and even the simple moments of stillness had converted into a profound realization—presence was no longer just a practice or a fleeting escape from the chaos of life.

Sitting in the quiet of his home, Aryan began to see presence as something far greater than a temporary reprieve from the high-stakes world he inhabited. Presence, he realized, was the very essence of life itself.

Gone were the days when Aryan viewed success solely through the lens of ambition, status, and accolades. The Ferrari, once a gleaming emblem of his ego-driven aspirations, had taken on a new meaning. It was no longer just a trophy symbolizing the heights he had scaled in the corporate world. Now, every drive in that car became an opportunity to reconnect with the present. With his hands on the wheel, Aryan was no longer racing toward an elusive future; he was fully grounded in the beauty of the moment.

The world around him—the road, the trees, the sky—came alive in ways he had never noticed before.

As the landscape changed outside the windows, so too did the landscape within Aryan. He realized that his transformation wasn't about rejecting ambition but about integrating it with the peace that comes from being present. The Ferrari, once a symbol of outward achievement, had become a metaphor for his inner journey—a reminder that both ambition and tranquility could coexist beautifully.

Presence was no longer a destination to be reached after the work was done or when life slowed down. It wasn't something he could 'achieve' and then set aside. Instead, presence was a continuous, evolving practice—an ongoing dance between awareness and experience. It was about being fully awake to the richness of life in every moment, regardless of whether he was in the boardroom, at home with his family, or simply enjoying a quiet drive.

Presence had taught Aryan that life wasn't about the endpoint, nor was it about the accolades or the external validations. True success lay in the ability to remain centered, to find peace in the present moment, and to understand that fulfillment wasn't tied to any single achievement or milestone. It could be found in the quiet in-between moments—the pauses, the breaths, the simple acts of awareness.

Aryan felt a deep sense of peace - Presence had given him the ability to reflect on his achievements without attachment, to appreciate the process of becoming without being consumed by the outcome.

Sitting quietly at home, Aryan smiled, assured that no matter where his journey led, he would move forward grounded in the present. With each step, he would carry the lessons of mindfulness, peace, and balance, paving the way for a future where ambition and tranquility could coexist in harmony.

Multiple Paths, One Destination

"In the end, the journey's essence lies not in the external path we take but in the inner transformation we undergo."

Aryan Kapoor nestled into the luxurious leather seat of his Ferrari, the gentle purring of the engine creating a soothing backdrop to his swirling thoughts - the city lights sparkled like stars, casting a vibrant mosaic of colors across the sleek dashboard—a reflection of the dynamic world that had once consumed him entirely. Tonight, the city was more than just a bustling expanse; it was a canvas of his transformation, painted with bold strokes of ambition, introspection, and newfound balance.

Reflecting on the Journey

For Aryan, the Ferrari had transformed from a mere status symbol—once embodying his relentless pursuit of success and validation—into a profound reminder of his personal evolution. In the past, it represented wealth and power, fueling his ego and ambition. But as he cruised through the vibrant city streets, the car now reflected a journey that took him from dizzying heights to deep self-reflection, culminating in a renewed sense of purpose and peace.

This transformation was not instantaneous; it unfolded gradually through moments of doubt, contemplation, and growth. Aryan learned that true fulfillment wasn't about abandoning material possessions but redefining his relationship with them. Instead of viewing wealth and success as burdens, he embraced them as tools to enrich his life.

He realized that inner peace could coexist with the enjoyment of his achievements. This shift in perspective allowed him to see the Ferrari not just as a status symbol but as a testament to his journey toward balance, mindfulness, and the joyful integration of ambition and serenity.

With every turn of the wheel, Aryan felt a surge of clarity. His path was uniquely his own; he didn't have to choose between material success and spiritual fulfillment. Instead, he could cultivate a harmonious relationship with both, uncovering the beauty of living fully in each moment while remaining anchored in the present.

Ferrari - A Moment of Realization

As Aryan navigated deeper into the city's vibrant core, the soft roar of the Ferrari's engine filled him with clarity. He realized that inner peace wasn't a distant destination but a profound state of being.

He understood that he didn't have to give up his Ferrari or his fast-paced lifestyle to find this peace. Instead, he could harmoniously blend both worlds, embracing his material desires alongside his spiritual aspirations.

The Ferrari had transformed from a mere possession into a symbol of his balanced life. It now served as a powerful reminder that true inner peace comes from within, shaped by personal growth rather than external circumstances. Once a vessel of ego and ambition, the car was now a steadfast companion, reflecting the equilibrium Aryan had achieved.

Conclusion

As Aryan's journey draws to a close, it becomes clear that the path to fulfillment is not about choosing one life over another, but about embracing the full spectrum of existence. The lessons he learned—finding harmony between ambition and tranquility, material success and spiritual growth—are universal truths applicable to us all.

In a world often divided between extremes, Aryan's story is a testament to the possibility of integration. It inspires us to explore our own journeys, encouraging us to seek balance in our lives. As we close this chapter, may we each remember that true peace and fulfillment lie not in renunciation but in the thoughtful melding of our aspirations, allowing us to thrive in both our inner and outer worlds.

Author's Note

Dear Readers,

As you reach the end of this journey with Aryan Kapoor, I want to take a moment to share my reflections and express my gratitude.

Writing *I Luv my Ferrari* has been an incredibly rewarding experience.

My hope is that Aryan's journey has offered you a fresh perspective on the interplay between ambition and inner peace, illustrating that one does not have to abandon their desires or possessions to achieve true contentment.

Throughout this book, we've traveled with Aryan as he navigated the complex landscape of modern life, seeking a balance between his aspirations and his quest for deeper meaning. His story serves as a reminder that peace and fulfillment are not necessarily found in renunciation or drastic life changes but can be cultivated through mindfulness, perspective shifts, and a harmonious relationship with our material world.

The ultimate lesson from Aryan's journey—and from the inspirations that guided it—is that there are myriad paths to the same destination. It's not the external circumstances but the internal transformation that defines our spiritual journey. As you close the final pages, I encourage you to reflect on your own life and consider how you might integrate the principles of mindfulness and balance into your daily routines and ambitions.

Thank you for joining me on this exploration. Your engagement with Aryan's story has been deeply appreciated, and I hope the insights shared within these pages will serve you as you navigate your own path toward peace and fulfillment.

Remember, the journey to inner peace is not a destination but a continuous process of growth and self-discovery.

With heartfelt thanks and best wishes,

Santanu Saxenaa

Author's Personal Note

Dear Reader,

As I share this book with you, I want to take a moment to express my heartfelt gratitude for joining me on this journey. This is my very first endeavor into the world of writing, and I can't tell you how exhilarating—and a bit daunting—it has been.

As an avid reader, I have always been inspired by the power of words, but I often struggled to find my own voice in written expression. It was a challenge that held me back for quite some time. However, through the power of AI, I discovered a way to articulate my thoughts and feelings in a way that resonated with me. This technology has become a vital tool, allowing me to find the words I need to express myself.

This book is a blend of my thoughts and experiences, aided by the incredible capabilities of AI. The content you see is both AI-assisted and AI-generated, which has empowered me to bring my ideas to life in a way I hadn't been able to before. I hope this unique collaboration translates into something that resonates with you, inspiring your own reflections and insights.

Your feedback is invaluable to me, and I would love to hear your thoughts on this book. Please feel free to reach out to me via any social medium listed.

Thank you for being a part of this adventure. I look forward to hearing from you and navigating this journey together.

Warm regards,

Santanu Saxenaa

Warrior Pose II – Virabhadrasana II (veer-ah-bah-DRAHS-anna)

Pose Description

Warrior Pose II is named after Virabhadra, a fierce warrior incarnation of the Hindu god Shiva. In Warrior II, bend your front knee deeply while extending your arms  straight from the shoulders, parallel to the ground. Keep your gaze, or drishti, focused on your front hand. This posture represents strength, stamina, focus, and courage.

Benefits and Focus

Warrior II enhances physical endurance and sharpens mental focus. By maintaining awareness of your sensations, you learn to discern between physical necessity and psychological desire. This mindfulness teaches the discipline of a true warrior.

Philosophical Insight

Warrior II is a practice in mental fortitude. Embracing discomfort with focus strengthens resilience and clarity, aligning body and mind with your spiritual goals, creating a balance between physical effort and inner intention.

Mountain Pose - Tadasana (tah-DAHS-anna)

Pose Description

Tadasana, or Mountain Pose, is the foundation of all standing yoga poses. While seemingly simple, it requires precise alignment and grounding. Stand tall with your feet together, pressing through all four corners. Engage your thighs, lift your chest, and keep your arms relaxed at your sides with palms facing forward. Maintain a soft, steady gaze ahead.

Benefits and Focus

Mountain Pose improves posture, balance and alignment while enhancing body awareness and mindfulness. Though physically subtle, it fosters a deep connection to the earth, reminding you that true strength comes from stillness and presence.

Philosophical Insight

Tadasana teaches us to stay grounded and resilient, like a mountain enduring the seasons. It helps transcend mental distractions, cultivating inner strength and harmony between body and spirit.

Child's Pose - Balasana
(bah-LAHS-anna)

Pose Description:

Balasana, or Child's Pose, is a calming and restorative posture. Begin by kneeling, then sit back on your heels and fold forward,  resting your forehead on the mat. Arms can extend in front or rest beside your body, allowing complete surrender and relaxation.

Benefits and Focus:

Child's Pose soothes stress, fatigue, and tension, creating a sense of security and reconnection with the breath. It offers a retreat from external demands and mental distractions, serving as a reminder of the importance of rest and rejuvenation in our fast-paced lives.

Philosophical Insight:

Balasana represents humility and letting go. Like a child returning to safety, the pose teaches that surrendering is a necessary path to healing and inner peace, fostering trust in oneself and the universe.

Tree Pose - Vrksasana
(Vrik-SHAHS-anna)

Pose Description

Vrksasana, or Tree Pose, is a balancing posture symbolizing stability and growth. Stand firmly on one foot, placing the opposite foot against your inner thigh or calf. Hands can be in prayer position at the chest or extended upward, reaching for the sky. Keep your gaze calm and steady to maintain balance.

Benefits and Focus

Tree Pose strengthens the legs and core while enhancing focus and concentration. Balancing on one leg encourages inner stability amid external challenges. The pose reflects personal growth, teaching you to stay rooted while reaching toward spiritual goals. With practice, maintaining balance becomes easier as trust in oneself grows.

Philosophical Insight

Vrksasana emphasizes the balance between effort and ease, grounding and rising. Life's challenges are like winds swaying a tree, but when deeply rooted, one can weather any storm while still aspiring to grow. The pose symbolizes alignment with your spiritual goals—firmly grounded yet ever-reaching upward.

Corpse Pose - Shavasana
(shah-VAHS-anna)

Pose Description:

Shavasana, or Corpse Pose, is traditionally practiced at the end of a yoga session to absorb the benefits of the practice. In this pose, you lie flat on your back with arms  relaxed by your sides, palms facing upward. The body remains completely still, and the focus shifts to deep breathing and inner awareness.

Benefits and Focus:

Shavasana promotes deep relaxation and helps restore balance. It soothes the nervous system and quiets the mind. Initially, it can be challenging to let go as thoughts surface. However, over time, you learn that Shavasana is about simply being— letting go of control and resting in the present moment.

Philosophical Insight:

Shavasana represents the death of the ego and the birth of deeper awareness. In this stillness, profound clarity arises as you realize that peace comes from releasing attachment to outcomes and embracing the present. In this pose, body, mind, and spirit align, allowing for complete integration of what has been learned on the mat and in life.

Acknowledgments

To Robin Sharma, the brilliant author of *The Monk Who Sold His Ferrari*, I extend my deepest gratitude and heartfelt thanks. Your book has been a beacon of inspiration and a profound source of wisdom for countless readers, including myself. The story of the protagonist has resonated deeply, sparking transformative insights in many.

Your narrative of self-discovery, simplicity, and spiritual enlightenment provided a foundation for my own exploration of these themes, albeit from a different perspective. It prompted me to consider how one might achieve similar spiritual fulfillment without stepping away from the world's luxuries and ambitions.

In *I Luv My Ferrari*, I sought to explore this very concept. Inspired by your profound teachings, I delved into the journey of Aryan Kapoor, a character who, while embracing the material world and its successes, strives to achieve inner peace and balance. The essence of your book influenced key aspects of Aryan's journey—particularly his reflections and the pursuit of a deeper understanding of true peace.

Your story served as a catalyst for my own narrative, leading me to investigate how one can integrate spiritual practices into a life filled with ambition and material success.

The principles and insights from *The Monk Who Sold His Ferrari* helped shape Aryan's path, illustrating that peace and mindfulness are not confined to a life of renunciation but can be cultivated amidst modern life's chaos.

Thank you for your invaluable contribution to this journey. Your work has not only inspired my book but has also enriched my understanding of the balance between material wealth and spiritual growth. It is my hope that *I Luv My Ferrari* honors the spirit of your teachings while offering a fresh perspective for those navigating their own paths to inner peace amidst a world of ambition.

I want to clarify that my intent is not to malign you or your book in any way; I humbly apologize in case my views and approach offend your book or your views in any manner. I sincerely hope that my exploration of these themes is received in the spirit of inspiration and growth.

With deep respect and appreciation,

– Santanu Saxenaa

Reader's Journal

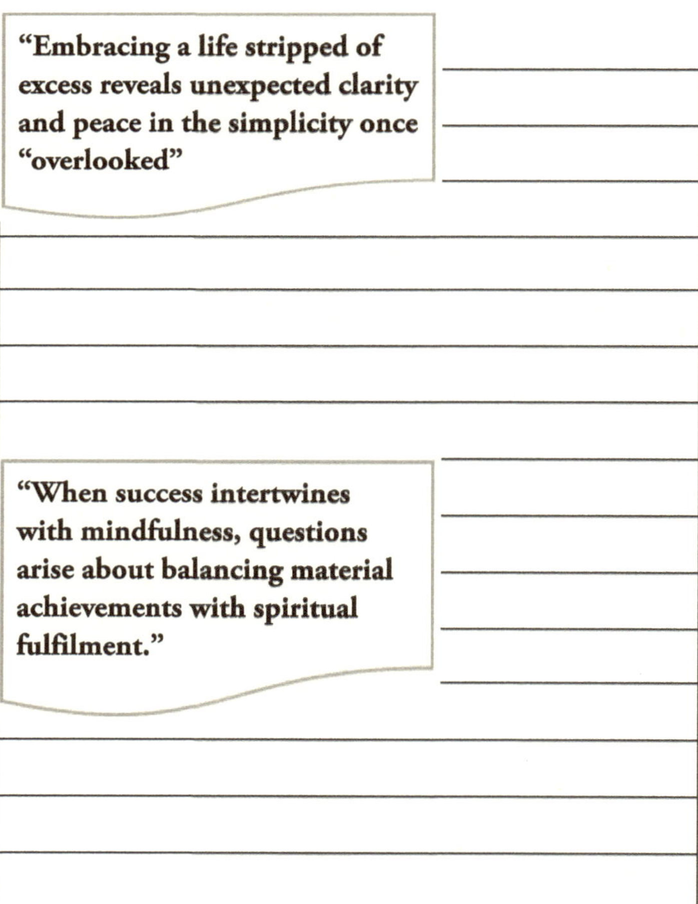

"To master the world, one must first master oneself"

"Daily practices of gratitude shift the focus from what is lacking to what is abundant, fostering a sense of fulfilment"